HIKING IN THE NORTHEASTERN UNITED STATES

Yves Séguin

2nd Edition

D1611687

ULYSSES
TRAVEL PUBLICATIONS
Travel better... enjoy more

Series Director Claude Morneau	*English Editor* Jennifer McMorran	*Layout* Christian Roy Isabelle Lalonde
Project Supervisor Pascale Couture	*English Translation* Jennifer McMorran Tracy Kendrick Eric Hamovitch	*Artistic Director* Patrick Farei Atoll Direction
Research and *Composition* Yves Séguin	*Cartography* André Duchesne	*Photography* Cover
Collaboration Sylvain Geneau	*Illustrations* Jean-François Bienvenue	Mount Mansfield Martin Kuhnigh Reflexion

Thanks to: Alain Poirier, Physical Education professor at the Université du Québec à Montràl; Marc Blais, adventurer, producer and televeision host for Productions la Sterne; Marie-Josée Guy, for f-reading and moral support.

Ulysses Travel Publications thanks SODEC and the Canadian Heritage Ministry for their financial support.

Distributors

AUSTRALIA:
Little Hills Press
11/37-43 Alexander St.
Crows Nest NSW 2065
☎ (612) 437-6995
Fax: (612) 438-5762

GERMANY & AUSTRIA:
Brettschneider
Fernreisebedarf GmbH
Hauptstr. 5
85586 Poing bei
München
☎ 08121-71436
Fax: 08121-71419

NETHERLANDS:
Nilsson & Lamm
Pampuslaan 212-214
1380 AD Weesp (NL)
☎ 02940-65044
Fax: 02940-15054

SPAIN:
Altaïr
Balmes 69
E-08007 Barcelona
☎ (34-3) 323-3062
Fax: (3403) 451-2559

CANADA:
Ulysses Books & Maps
4176 Saint-Denis
Montréal, Québec
H2W 2M5
☎ (514) 843-9882, x. 2232
Fax: 514-843-9448

GREAT BRITAIN &
IRELAND:
World Leisure Marketing
9 Downing Road West
Meadows, Derby
UK DE21 6HA
☎ 1 332 343 332
Fax: 1 332 340 464

SCANDINAVIA:
Scanvik
Esplanaden 8B
Copenhagen K
DK-1263
☎ 33.12.77.66
Fax: 33.91.28.82

SWITZERLAND:
OLF
P.O. Box 1061
CH-1701 Fribourg
☎ 41.37.83.51.11
Fax: 41.37.26.63.60

BELGIUM:
Vander
Vrijwilligerlaan 321
B-1150 Brussel
☎ (02) 762 98 04
Fax: (02) 762 06 62

ITALY:
Edizioni del Riccio
Via di Soffiano 164 A
50143 Firenze
☎ (055) 71 63 50
Fax: (055) 71 33 33

SOUTH-EAST ASIA
Graham Brash
32 Gul Drive
Singapore 2262
☎ 65.86.11.336
Fax: 65.86.14.815

U.S.A.:
Seven Hills Book
Distributors
49 Central Avenue
Cincinnati, Ohio, 45202
☎ 1-800-545-2005
Fax: (513) 381-0753

Other countries, contact Ulysses Books & Maps (Montréal), Fax : (514) 843-9448

Séguin, Yves, 1961-
    Hiking in the Northeastern United States
    2nd ed.
    (Ulysses green escapes)
    Translation of: Randonnée pédestre nord-est des États-Unis
    Includes index
    ISBN 2-89464-010-2

1. Hiking - New England - Guidebooks. 2. New England - Guidebooks. I. Title. II. Series.
GV199.42.N68S4313 1996   796.5'1'0974   C96-940558-8

© August 1996, Ulysses Travel Publications
All rights reserved
ISBN 2-89464-010-2

"The swiftest traveller is he that goes afoot."

Walden
Henri David Thoreau

ABOUT THE AUTHOR

Hiking, cross-country skiing, rock-climbing, cycling... for the last twelve years, Yves Séguin has had a hand in everything to do with the great outdoors. He has worked as a researcher for the French-language television show *Oxygène*, and since 1995 he has written numerous articles for the French-language magazines *Espaces* and *Geo Plein air* and as a correspondant for the newspaper *La Presse*.

Yves is also the author of *Hiking in Quebec* (Ulysses Travel Publications), and has worked as an instructor for the orienteering and hiking courses offered by the *Fédération québécoise de la marche*.

Yves was born in 1961 in Laval, north of Montréal. He has a bachelor's degree (1990) in physical education from the Université du Québec à Montréal as well as a certificate (1994) in educational sciences from the same school.

TABLE OF CONTENTS

LIST OF MAPS

Help make Ulysses Travel Guides even better!

The information contained in this guide was correct at press time. However, mistakes can slip in, omissions are always possible, places can disappear, etc. The authors and publisher hereby disclaim any liability for loss or damage resulting from omissions or errors.

We value your comments, corrections and usggestions, as they allow us to keep each guide up to date. The best contributions will be rewarded with a free book from Ulysses Travel Publications. All you have to do is write us at the following address and indicate which title you would be interested in receiving. (see the list at end of guide).

Ulysses Travel Publications
4176 Rue Saint-Denis
Montréal, Québec
Canada H2W 2M5

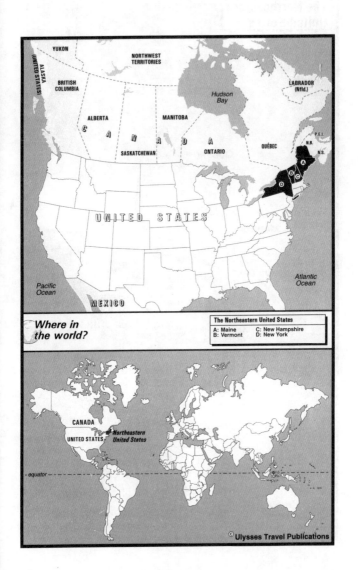

Where in the world?

The Northeastern United States	
A: Maine	C: New Hampshire
B: Vermont	D: New York

© Ulysses Travel Publications

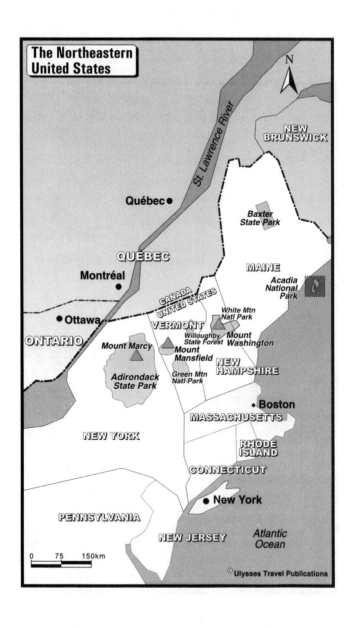

The Northeastern United States

INTRODUCTION

The aim of this hiking guide is to help hikers of all kinds discover the most beautiful and picturesque trails in the northeastern United States. As such, not every walking and hiking area is included, only a carefully selected, well trodden few.

We have included three of the six states which make up New England: Maine, New Hampshire, Vermont, as well as New York State.

While providing important information for beginners (distances, times, costs, reservations, food, safety and rescue, etc.), this guide also informs the experienced hiker with an extensive choice of lesser known, but very interesting trails.

We have listed the most spectacular sites located within a few hours' drive of the larger centres in the northeastern United States and eastern Canada. Hiking is far and away the best way to discover, experience and explore this region of the northeastern United States. One-hundred and thirty-four hiking trails, covering more than 1,120 km of trails thus await your footprints.

Happy Trails to You... ♪ ♫

Since the dawn of time, human beings have gotten around by walking. Man is said to have started walking close to three million years ago. Whether it was to head off to the hunt and to gather, to wage war against the enemy, to herd animals up into mountain pastures, to make a pilgrimmage or simply to get to work or to better oneself, walking has always been central to man's mobility.

It was not until the 18th century, however, that walking became something to watch. Endurance walks were organized mostly in England. Various tests of endurance became all the rage, in one of these 100 miles had to be covered in less than 24 hours, a feat accomplished in 1762 in 23 hours and 15 minutes. Other events stretched out over several days, with spectators cheering along the way. Records like 400 miles in six days, 700 miles in 14 days and 1000 miles in 1000 hours were set and remain awesome performances.

Mountain walking goes all the way back to Roman times. At the time various trails (Roman roads) were laid to traverse European mountains passes. These trails along with many other mountain paths were also used (and still are) for shepherding animals up to high mountain pastures. Many of these are now the most spectacular hiking trails.

Hiking in the northeastern United States is certainly nothing new. The first trails were cleared more than 150 years ago. The highest summits of each state quickly intrigued the first explorers, not to mention that they had already been well covered by the natives who named them in order to give them life.

At the end of the 19th century, several summit houses were built in the mountains to lodge fanatics of this new activity. Sick people were also brought to these places by doctors who sought to revitalize them with the clean crisp mountain air.

In the early 1900s, hiking became more and more fashionable. Associations and groups were formed as the activity of walking became more structured and established. The first trail guides were published at this time as well. In New Hampshire, the Appalachian Mountain Club published the first edition of the *AMC White Mountain Guide* in 1907; ten years later the Green Mountain Club of Vermont put out its famous *Long Trail Guide* which describes the route of this 437-km-long linear track! And in the Adirondacks, in the state of New York, the first edition of the **Guide to Adirondack Trails/High Peaks Region** saw the light in 1934 thanks to the work of the Adirondack Mountain Club.

Hiking and Walking Clubs

People usually hike with family or in couples. There are, however, several hiking clubs that organize excursions in the northeastern United States. There are two main reasons people join hiking clubs, first of all to get motivated and force themselves to just get up and go, and secondly to meet people who share the same interest in physical activity.

It is best to shop around for the right club, since there are clubs for all tastes; walking in the city, walking indoors, speed-walking, endurance hiking, mountain hiking, excursions, clubs for singles, for the elderly, etc. Certain clubs offer various different activities including transportation, others opt for car-pooling, which can significantly reduce costs.

It is interesting to note that many clubs organize evening city walks during the week. Some walkers will take advantage of these for the sake of getting out, while for others it is an opportunity to train for mountain hikes. These excursions are inexpensive and contribute to good physical fitness by maintaining a steady pace (usually about 6 km/h), plus they are a great way to make new friends.

In Quebec, the *Fédération québécoise de la marche* at ☎ (514) 252-3157 can inform on hiking clubs in the province. Many colleges and universities also have outdoors clubs that organize hiking excursions.

As far as local clubs are concerned, these are listed at the beginnning of each chapter. Formed many years ago, these dynamic clubs usually have several regional chapters in their particular state offering courses, presentations, environmental education, volunteer programs, publications, etc.

■ Starting a Hiking Club

Many people prefer to start their own hiking club. With the help of a few friends it is relatively easy to delegate the jobs: car-pooling, safety, telephone numbers and calling, food etc. The bigger the club gets the more planning and confirming are required.

Quiz: Hiking in the Northeastern United States

True or False:

1. The Long Trail traverses New Hampshire from north to south.

2. The summit of Mount Washington is enshrouded in cloud 300 days a year.

3. Taking care of your feet also involves keeping your toenails short and cut square.

4. Katahdin is an Indian word that means "mountain of spirits".

5. The state of New Hampshire is called the Granite State.

6. If a blister forms while hiking it should be pierced and drained.

7. The state of New York is the most populous state of the New England states.

8. Proteins play a role in the body's structure.

9. Arctic-alpine vegetation is only found on three summits in Vermont.

10. The Green Mountain only accepts members who have hiked the entire Long Trail.

11. Wool conserves heat, even when wet.

12. The first trail to the top of Mount Marcy was cleared in 1921.

13. Hypothermia starts when the body temperature falls below the freezing point.

14. Algonquin Peak is the third highest summit in the Adirondacks.

15. Mount Hunger is part of the Worcester chain.

16. The second layer of clothing is meant to preserve the body's humidity.

17. The Camel's Hump is located in the Adirondacks.

18. The Appalachian Trail is 3,460 km long.

19. A leather gourd is by far the preferred water carrier of experienced hikers.

20. A luge and bobsleigh track winds its way down the north face of Mount Van Hoevenberg.

21. Acadia National Park is located on an island.

22. The temperature drops 5°C with each 100 m of altitude gained.

23. The Abenaki Indians called Mount Mansfield "Tah-wak-be-dee-ee-wadso".

24. A lean-to is a steep incline.

25. Equidistance is the change in altitude between contour lines.

26. The world record of wind velocity, recorded at the summit of Mount Washington in 1934, was 370 km/h.

27. When buying hiking boots, make sure your heel moves freely.

28. The Swedish trekker Ingmar Trek invented high mountain hiking, now called trekking.

29. If it is 5°C and the wind is blowing 50 km/h, the actual temperature (what your skin senses) will be -12°C.

30. The Long Trail, which leads from Mount Mansfield to the Camel's Hump is closed in spring.

Answers on page 227.

HIKING

Hiking is an aerobic activity; it is therefore normal for breathing to fluctuate at the beginning of a hike, as the amount of oxygen being consumed is increasing rapidly. When consumption of oxygen stabilizes so do breathing and heart rate.

The physical benefits of hiking are obvious. First of all, at the cardio-vascular level, the size and capacity of the heart increase. As a result, the volume of blood pumped through the body and the heart rate increase. Even though the resting heart rate decreases, the amount of oxygen supplied to the body actually increases because the heart is able to distribute blood to active muscles more efficiently.

Aerobic training reduces systolic and diastolic pressures (blood pressure) at rest and during light exercise, particularly among those with hyper-tension. Over time these developments allow us to do the same hike again and again, each time feeling better than the last.

Most health experts (doctors, physical educators, physiotherapists, kinesiotherapists, etc.) agree that walking is the most complete and least hamrful exercise. Several muscle groups (legs, abdominal, chest) are used as are most joints. It is widely accepted that the more the heart, muscles, bones and joints are used the more adequately they function, and the slower they age.

The psychological benefits of hiking are less obvious, but no less significant. Everyone who hikes or walks regularly (hiking on weekends and walking during the week) will notice positive changes in their outlook. In the outdoors a simple existence brings us in touch with nature and back to the basics. Meditation, observation, and clean crisp air all lead to a clear state of mind. We return from a hike refreshed, rejuvenated, and relaxed.

French climber Yves Pollet-Villard once said of the mountains, "Up there we find ourselves." Life seems simpler and more harmonious, far from the madding crowds of urban life, leaving the mind clear for endless possibilities.

Unlike more technically demanding sports, hiking does not require too much concentration, leaving the hiker free to meditate and reflect. Some of the best ideas are born out of this state of well-being. Not surprisingly, for some hikers, to walk every day is not only an obligation, but satisfies a profound need to come back to oneself.

The Physiology of Walking

Simply put, hiking is walking. That, however, is where the simplicity ends. There are countless ways of walking and countless different types of terrain to walk on. The amount of energy spent during a walk varies significantly with the walking surface. Just as walking on pavement is not at all like walking on snow or sand, so walking on the sidewalk is not at all like trekking over the rough terrain (mud, boulders, etc.) you will find on a mountain hike.

Walking or hiking can be practised in many different forms. Walking generally includes the sporty side of the activity, where improvements in technical form, physical conditioning and speed are sought; it has much more to do with the individual than the environment. Hiking, on the other hand, is different because of the "natural" aspect; in effect it is a means (and not an end) of locomotion that allows the hiker to visit various natural milieus. Hiking, therefore has much more to do with the surroundings than the individual. Of course, one does not preclude the other, and hiking can be very physically demanding, leading to an overall improvement of the hiker's level of physical fitness.

■ Different types of walking and hiking

Basic Walking: This is the kind of walking everyone does. With a relatively slow speed (3-4 km/h), basic walking will not improve the level of physical fitness, but will help maintain it.

Rhythmic Walking: This kind of walking requires a greater physical effort than the latter. Rhythmic walking (5-6 km/h) is required in order to improve level of physical fitness. Once used to rhythmic walking, a hiker can easily walk long distances without getting too tired.

Fast walking: Fast walking (6-8 km/h) is a sport and requires some getting used to. Body movement is much more dynamic and the heart rate is much faster. Fast walking is just as beneficial as running and avoids its downfalls (impact injuries).

Speed Walking: Speed walking requires a much more precise and technical form as well as an excellent level of physical fitness. Speed walking (8-15 km/h) also allows an athlete to measure him or herself against other walkers at organized competitions.

Hiking: Hiking leads walkers into the forest, to the mountains, across fields or through any natural milieu. Mpt at all concerned with speed, hiking does present its share of complications related to changes in altitude and type of terrain (grass, sand, mud, snow, etc.). Experienced hikers generally end adopting a style that resembles rhythmic walking.

Long Hike: This type of hiking allows the hiker to spend sveral consecutive days in the forest or mountains. The biggest consideration here is carrying a heavy backpack.

Trekking: Trekking is essentially a long hike in a remote wilderness area. A trek usually lasts more than a week and is often combines exotic travel, adventure and altitude. The Himalayas are without a doubt the ultimate trekking destination in the world.

Alpine: Alpine hiking is inextricably related to mountaineering because of the special equipment required (crampons, leggings, rope, ice axe, etc.) And the special knownledge of the dangers of mountain require (avalanche, altitude acclimatization, etc.). This kind of hiking is nevertheless accessible to all hikers in good physical consition. The Canadian and American Rocky Mountains, the Apls and the Pyrenees offer countless summits to scale.

Short and Long Hikes: The terms long and short hikes, as they are used in this guide, do not refer to the total distance covered. A "short hike" is one where the hiker returns to the starting point to sleep and so carries only a day pack containing lunch, water, sweater, anorak, camera, etc. A "long hike" involves an overnight somewhere along the trail. The hiker must therefore carry all the essentials for two or more days, (food, clothing, campstove, mess-kit, sleeping-bag, tent, etc.). "Short hikes" can still be quite demanding. Imagine, for example, more than 30 km of hiking in one day with considerable change of altitude, a "long hike" on the other hand, covering a short distance over unchanging terrain, would be much easier.

■ Ways of Walking

Hiking in the mountains involves, aside from the occasional flat stretch, walking uphill and walking downhill.

Flat terrain: It is important to develop good habits when walking. Dragging your feet with a hunched back and eyes to the ground is not the most efficient way to hike. Since walking involves a continual shift of your centre of gravity forward, good posture is imperative. Keep your head up, back straight, swing your arms and your upper body extended. Knees should never be completely extended (except in speed-walking). Your heel should touch the ground first, and remember that it is better to take longer strides than several shorter steps.

Walking Uphill: Unlike walking on a flat surface, where the oscillation of the centre of gravity is what propels us forward, walking uphill requires a constant push against gravity. The foot has a tendency to place itself flat and directly below the centre of gravity. This position requires that the ankle be fully extended and often results in shin pain or injury. The upper body leans forward in an effort to balance the centre of gravity. The muscles of the knee and hips also have to work harder in order to carry the hiker uphill against gravity.

Walking Downhill: Going downhill requires a constant braking against gravity. This "negative" work puts an enormous strain on the muscles and tendons of the leg. The centre of gravity must be kept behind the forward leg, which requires leaning the body back, slowing down the descent. The leg must be moved forward slowly until it touches the ground and then, by bending the knee, the centre of gravity is carefully shifted downwards. Since walking downhill requires this constant braking with the lower body, it is often much more strenuous on the muscles than walking uphill. Running downhill, especially when carrying a backpack, is not recommended and can even be dangerous.

■ Carrying a Load

Usually the hikers are carrying not only their own weight up and down-hill. And there is a significant difference between a day-hike with a backpack and several days of hiking where you are carrying all your equipment on your back. Longer hikes can mean up to 25 kg of extraweight. A day-pack, on the other hand can weigh up to 7 kg, which can have an impact on the energy expended during a day. The weight of hiking shoes can also make quite a difference, since it takes much more energy to carry extra weight on the feet than on the upper body.

■ Rhythm

Experienced hikers know how to pace themselves. It is important to remember not to set out on a trail too fast, yet to maintain a pace that requires some exertion. Do not give up at the smallest sign of fatigue. Allow some time for your body to adjust to the physical demands being placed on it.

Being out of breath occurs when the amount of air inhaled (oxygen) is less than that which is exhaled (carbon dioxide). During prolonged exertion, the lungs have trouble absorbing enough air to satisfy their need for oxygen. The hiker inhales faster, but does not necessarily also exhale faster, leaving more vitiated air in the lungs. Over a steep incline, therefore the hiker should concentrate on exhaling.

Getting out of breath generally means a lack of training or a pace that was too quick for the physical capacity of the moment. To avoid this, the hiker should start out slower and work up to a quicker pace.

Experience will also help each hiker develop his or her own rhythm with respect to taking breaks. Most experts advise a ten minute resting period after each hour of walking. Try not to stop every fifteen minutes since at that rate the body does not have a chance to adjust to the exertion. During a hike, snacks and especially water are a must. You should be drinking almost continuously even if you're not thirsty, so practise walking and drinking at the same time.

Smoking

Smoking while walking is a real no-brainer when it comes to your cardiovascular system. Nevertheless, it is comon to see people walking with a cigarette in their mouth. If they succeed in walking and smoking at the same time, it is because their pace has been slowed down. A smoker who wants to quit should pick up the pace (5-6 km/h) to a point where hiking and smoking at the same time are impossible. Perhaps they'll be encouraged to leave the cigarettes at home next time, or maybe even for good.

Furthermore, countless forest fires, even near urban areas are started by smoldering cigarettes. Smoking hikers should always bring along a portable ashtray for the ashes and butts, or they should simply not smoke while hiking.

Training

Arriving at the summit of a mountain is much more pleasant if you are not tired and out of breath. You will appreciate the break much more, eat with a hearty appetite, relax and look forward to the hike down.

Physical fitness is essential to enjoying and appreciating a good hike, and to eventually attempting some more difficult ones. It is not necessary to train intensively three hours a day, lift weights, or follow a strictly regimented diet. There are many little tricks that will help you build up physical endurance.

The essential is of course walking. Walking three times a week for an hour each time, maintaining a relatively quick pace, (but not so fast as to make conversation impossible) is the best way to train. Within a couple of weeks you will easily quicken your pace and walk comfortably even with a loaded backpack.

Activities like biking, jogging, cycling and cross-country skiing are all aerobic activities and therefore also excellent ways to train for hiking. A good way to make your work-outs more effective is to vary their length, frequency and intensity. Short excursions at a fast pace are just as effective.

Some simple changes to your daily routine will actually make a significant difference to your level of physical fitness. If possible try walking or riding a bike to work. Walk to the grocery store and, if the bags are too heavy use a backpack. Take the stairs instead of the elevator. Take a short walk after eating lunch. Watch television while riding a stationary bike. Every little bit helps.

■ Heart Rate

The average resting heart rate is 70 beats per minute. A less active person's resting rate will probably be closer to 90 beats per minute, while for those in top physical shape it may be as low as 40 beats per minute. In order to read your heart rate, press your index and middle finger softly against your neck (carotid artery), temple (temporal artery) or wrist (radial artery), and count the number of beats for 15 seconds then multiply this number of four.

Keep in mind that your heart has a miximum heart rate (FCmax++) and that for aerobic exercise to be effective it must cause your heart rate to reach 70% to 90% of this FCmax++. Below 70% and the improvements will be minimal, above 90% and the strain put on your heart is considerable.

To find out your maximum heart rate (FCmax), subtract your age from 220. For example, for a 35-year old: 220 - 35 = 185 (FCmax++).

It is recommended to train to a rate between 70% and 90% of your FCmax++, a few simple calculations will give you this range: 70% of 185 (FCmax) = 130 beats per minute, and 90% of 185 (FCmax) = 167 beats per minute. Therefore a work-out that raises the heart rate to between 130 and 167 beats per minute (for a 35-year-old) will lead to an overall improvement in the level of physical fitness.

■ Always warm-up beforehand

Once the boots are laced up and the trail is picked, we're often in too much of a hurry to head out and get the blood flowing. But before taking off with cold and stiff muscles, it is imperative that you take a short ten minutes to warm up your body to avoid any injuries, aches or pains. It is better to warm up outside just before you start. A few stretching and flexibility exercises, and a slower pace at the start will increase your body temperature and agility.

The stretching should begin at the head and work its way down to the feet. It should be done gently and should not be painful. Muscles should be fully relaxed and loose at the time. Extend the muscle for a full 15 seconds, then release it slowly. To prepare your body, rotate the head, stretch the neck, rotate the shoulders, stretch the shoulders and arms, rotate the trunk, stretch the lower back, hips, thighs, calves, rotate the ankles and stretch the Achilles tendon.

After the hike, a few stretching and flexibility exercises will help reduce the risk of stiff muscles down the road.

■ Body Temperature

Normal body temperature is 37°C (96°F). While hiking, this temperature is maintained by putting on and taking off excess clothing, by drinking plenty of water, and by paying attention to your rhythm.

An experienced hiker will have no qualms about alerting their companions of any risks (heat stroke, hypothermia, etc.).

■ Foot Care

Feet are a hiker's most precious tool. If they hurt, the whole hike becomes painful. It only takes a small unattended blister to ruin a beautiful day in the woods. But caring for your feet requires a bit more than just carrying a few plastic bandages, just in case.

The foot is like a tripod with a series of shock absorbers. When the ligaments support all of the body's weight, they have a tendency to collapse, this is called flat-footedness. There are exercises that will counter this inconvenience by strengthening the muscles of the planter's arch, ask a doctor or orthopedist. Orthopedic soles can also be placed in your boots or shoes.

Taking care of your feet also involves keeping your toenails short and cut square, soaking your feet, keeping them clean and massaging them regularly. When you take a break while hiking take off your boots and socks to air out your feet. Check also that there are no blisters forming, and change sweaty socks.

Eating

A review of the basics tells us that a balanced diet is essential. The quality of the foods you take in on a daily basis influences your level of physical fitness. When hiking, food should be your first consideration. Heading out without any food is a big mistake that will almost certainly ruin your day, and potentially place you in danger.

Hiking promotes digestion and helps relieve constipation. The action of walking creates vibration in the body which gets things moving notably in the intestines, liver and pancreas, thereby ensuring regularity.

■ How Much Do You Need?

The amount of energy required by the body varies with age, sex, and the type of physical activity. Someone in their twenties burns about 2,200 calories during an average day. In the mountains, on a long hike, that same person will burn as many as 5,000 calories. It is therefore essential to eat more in order to compensate, but it is also essential to eat sensibly.

A healthy daily diet includes foods from the four foods groups:

- milk and dairy products (2 to 4 servings)
- breads and cereals (5 to 12 servings)
- meat and meat substitutes (2 to 3 servings)
- fruits and vegetables (5 to 10 servings)

■ What Do You Need?

Carbohydrates

Carbohydrates effectively provide the energy necessary for exertion. There are two types of carbohydrates: simple carbohydrates and complex carbohydrates. The first kind are found in sweets (chocolate, pastries, jams, etc.). Since they are digested by the body very quickly (one hour), they should make up only 10% of your daily intake of carbohydrates. Complex carbohydrates are found in foods like bread, pasta, rice, and grains. They are digested more slowly (two to six hours) and therefore provide a more constant source of energy. It is important to eat complex carbohydrates. They should make up approximately 55% of your daily intake of food.

Lipids

Lipids are either animal or vegetable fats. Animal fats should only make up one third of the total intake of fat, and vegetable fats the other two thirds. In total only 30-35% of the daily intake of calories should be from lipids. Animal fat is found in meats, butter, whole milk, cheese, and prepared foods like cold cuts. Vegetable fat is found in oils, margarine, nuts and chocolate. Lipids contribute significantly to the energy available to your body by protecting vital organs, maintaining body temperature, and transporting vitamins.

Proteins

Proteins are the building blocks of the body. They are responsible for the construction and repair of body tissue. They provide energy in extreme cases, such as malnutrition or fasting. As with lipids there are animal and vegetable proteins. Animal protein is found in meats and dairy products, while vegetable protein is found in cereals and legumes.

Minerals and Vitamins

Eating a balanced diet should take care of your vitamin and mineral needs. Excess vitamins are not stored in the body, but eliminated in the urine.

Water

While hiking, our bodies dehydrate at a much faster rate, and usually without our being aware of it. It is a good idea to get into the habit of drinking water regularly, even if you are not thirsty. Drink plenty of water before, during and after a hike to help your body rehydrate as quickly as possible. Each hiker should have their own one-litre water bottle. Water makes up 60% to 70% of body mass and has many functions: it regulates body temperature, transports minerals and vitamins and eliminates waste.

The body needs about 2.5 l of water per day. Since daily food intake will provide you with about 1 l of water does come from the daily food intake, you need to drink about 1.5 l of liquid (water, juice, etc.) per day. The body loses about 1 l of water (sweat) per hour while exercising.

In several regions of the northeastern United States, water sources are contaminated by the parasite *Giardia Lamblia* which causes intestinal problems like diarrhea. Many call it "Beaver Fever" because the parasite is carried into the water by beavers.

To avoid these symptoms, the water must be boiled for two to three minutes and treated with iodine tablets. One could also treat it by passing it through a filter designed for such purposes (this is effective but costly). For one-day hikes, carrying bottled water from home should suffice. Get in the habit of checking the water quality with the park staff, or the organization that manages the trails.

■ A Few Important Tips

- Food should be easy and quick to prepare (for ex. pre-cooked rice, instant oatmeal).
- Fruits and vegetables freeze quickly in the winter.
- Avoid meat during warm weather.
- Weight and volume should be minimized (get rid of as much packaging as possible, chop up vegetables ahead of time).
- Each meal should be individually wrapped.
- Starting a meal with hot soup is good idea since it will quickly replenish the salt and water lost during the day.
- The evening meal is important since your evening and next day depend on it.

■ Short Hikes

For a short hike of one day it is particularly important to ensure a high carbohydrate intake. Your body requires the energy immediately and carbohydrates provide it most effectively. Breakfast should be complete and well-balanced. Instead of stopping and eating a big lunch, snack along the way and during short breaks. "GORP" (good old raisins and peanuts) or trail-mix, a mixture of dried fruits and nuts, is a high-energy snack that can be munched on as you hike. Drinking a lot of water will also maximize your energy.

Suggestions

- Tomato and lettuce sandwiches
- dried or smoked meat (ham, salami, etc.)
- meatloaf or vegi-pate
- Chopped fresh vegetables (peppers, carrots, cauliflower, etc.)
- Fresh fruit (bananas don't do well in a backpack)
- Firm cheese
- Fruit or nut cake
- Trail mix, "GORP"
- Water or unsweetened juice

■ Long Hikes

On longer hikes a more balanced menu is necessary to avoid missing any essential nutrients. Priority should be given to carbohydrates since they provide about 60% of your daily calories and therefore 60% of your energy.

Suggestions

Breakfast:

- Oatmeal with brown sugar, powdered milk, and dried fruit
- Cream of wheat
- Muffins
- Pita bread, bagel, english muffin
- Peanut butter, jams, etc.
- Coffee, tea, hot chocolate

Lunch:

- Dried or sliced meats, vegi-pâté
- Cheddar cheese or cream cheese
- Heavy bread (bagel)

- Fresh and dried fruit
- Raw vegetables
- Fruit or nut cake
- Mixed nuts
- Fruit juice and water

Supper:

- Soup
- Vegetables and rice
- Couscous
- Pasta
- Cheese fondue
- Instant pudding
- Herbal tea or hot chocolate

Two books that wil help you plan outdoor meals are:

- *The Canada Food Guide*
- *The One-Pan Gourmet: Fresh Food on the Trail* by Cliff Jacobson, how to cook outdoors, plan meals, recipes, etc.

Walking and Weight Loss

A lot of people exercise with the sole purpose of losing weight. If this goal also leads them to the mountains, then all the better, since the most difficult part is getting into some sort of routine, actually getting out and daring to go. From the first few successful outings you will discover the benefits and joys of hiking.

Walking and hiking are excellent physical activities that promote weight loss. They require intensity and endurance, both of which are essential to controlling body weight. The intensity, or rhythm should be moderate (not too slow) and the duration of the activity quite long. This combination forces the body to draw the energy it requires from fat deposits in the body.

People who like to snack in between meals will find the following experiment interesting. The next time you feel hungry, go for a walk first. Once back from your walk not only will you feel more relaxed, you may even notice that you no longer feel hungry.

It has been found that hunger is often a result of higher stress levels. The difference between people with weight problems and those without is generally not an issue of how much food they eat, but rather how they spend their energy. Going on a strict diet is not sufficient to really bring your weight down; some sort of exercise is necessary.

If your diet is already well balanced, and you want to lose weight, cutting down your food intake is not a good idea. An increase in the intensity and regularity of exercise is more effective. The same principle holds for someone looking to maintain a specific weight.

First Aid

■ Typical Outdoor Injuries

It is important to be self-sufficient in the outdoors. As well as taking care of food, clothing, and shelter, you should also be equipped to handle any unforeseen snags — such as an accident that requires immediate attention. A first-aid kit is an indispensable tool to ensure that your hike is a safe one. It should be simple and contain only the material you are likely to need, appropriate to the kind of light injuries likely to occur during a hike, usually blisters and sprains.

Blisters

Blisters are most often the result of new shoes or of shoes that are too big. Before the blister actually develops, cover the area with a piece of moleskin (sold in pharmacies). If the blister has already formed, pierce it and drain out the liquid. This allows the blister to dry out and heal more quickly. It is important to disinfect the blister and surround it with moleskin to avoid any further rubbing and irritation.

Sprains

A sprained ankle occurs when the internal or external lateral ligaments are stretched. There are three types of sprains:

- A minor sprain is the most frequent type. The foot is twisted severely but there is no cracking sound nor immediate swelling. If the ankle is wrapped in a supportive bandage, the foot can be walked on until the closest rest area is reached. The pain will nonetheless be quite sharp.

The ankle should be iced as soon as possible. A cast is not necessary. In fact, the sooner one starts to walk on the ankle, the sooner it will heal itself.

- In the case of a moderate sprain the ligament is stretched and partially ripped. The cracking sound and inflammation that follow within the half hour make it easy to spot. The injured person will experience serious pain and will not be able to walk at all.

Ice or snow should be applied immediately and the injured person should be supported until a rest area is reached. The victim should stay off the injured ankle for 48 hours. On the third day the ankle, supported by a tensor bandage, can be walked on again.

- In a severe sprain the ligament is completely torn. The pain is intense and swelling occurs instantaneously. The injured person will be completely incapacitated, and the foot will turn blue immediately.

Before moving the injured person, immobilize the ankle. Support the person completely until a rest area is reached. A cast will be necessary and the injury may take several weeks to heal.

■ Stitches

While hiking, you may experience a sharp spasmodic pain in the side, this is called a stitch. If it happens on the left side it is because your spleen is contracting. If the pain is on the right side it is probably a diaphragmatic cramp caused by incorrect breathing. Slow down and breathe and exhale deeply. Stitches are common following a meal.

■ Hyperthermia and Hypothermia

Hyperthermia and hypothermia are caused by an imbalance of the body temperature. A hiker must maintain a normal body temperature of 37°C. If it rises above 38°C, then hyperthermia has begun, below 36°C and hypothermia has set in. Climactic conditions, physical exertion and hydration are all key factors in a hiker's body temperature.

Hyperthermia

Hyperthermia is an elevation of the body's normal temperature (37°C). It usually occurs during hot weather, and more specifically when it is very humid. The body loses water during physical exertion (up to 1 l per hour). This water which is transformed into sweat on the skin surface, evaporates and cools the skin. If too much water is lost, and not replaced by drinking liquids the body begins to dehydrate. Cramps, spasms and exhaustion may result.

If the body is not able to cool itslef and it is 30°C with 100% humidity, the body's internal temperature will rise above 37°C (up to 41°C). This is hyperthermia. If the body remains active after its cooling mechanism has broken down then "heatstroke" is imminent. Shivering, dizziness, headaches, sudden fatigue and even strange behaviour will begin. The body temperature must be lowered (find shade, remove clothing, apply ice or cold compress, etc.) And a doctor should be consulted.

During hot weather keep your head covered (hat, scarf, etc.) and drink a lot of liquids.

Hypothermia

Hypothermia starts when your internal body temperature falls below 36°C, as the body loses heat faster than it can produce it. Shivering is the first sign that your body is not able to warm itself. This sign should warn you to put on more clothing and to eat in order to replenish body's caloric energy.

Hypothermia is logically related to cold conditions. Winter, early spring and late fall weather nomally present the risk of hypothermia. It is easy to discount the cold when hiking in the month of July. However in the mountains, rain and wind can lower the temperature considerably. Imagine sitting above the tree line in a downpour, with the wind blowing at 50 km/h. Then imagine that you are tired and have no raincoat. In such conditions your body temperature will drop rapidly and you run the risk of hypothermia.

There are six stages of hypothermia.

Stage 1 (37°C to 35°C): beginning to shiver, stumbling or tripping without reason, reduced manual dexterity.

Stage 2 (35°C to 32°C): shivering is much more marked and speech is often interrupted by violent trembling; the pulse and breathing rate increase; the skin becomes pale.

Stage 3 (32°C to 30°C): blood pressure, pulse and breathing decrease; coordination of movement is difficult because of the increasing stiffness of the muscles, speech becomes confused and the victim will stumble.

Stage 4 (30°C to 27°C): confusion, incoherent thoughts, semi-consciousness, stiff muscles, and dilation of the pupils.

Stage 5 (27°C to 25°C): loss of consciousness, cardiac irregularities, and coma.

Stage 6 (less than 25°C): cardiac and respiratory failure, oedema and pulmonary hemorrhage. At this stage, the victim is not far from death.

Hypothermia is very serious. Even though the weather may not seem to present any risks, it is important to bring along enough food, water and warm clothing.

■ Frostbite

Winter hiking is very pleasant, but can be problematic if you aren't well prepared against the intense cold and violent wind.

Frostbite is a lesion caused by exposure to cold. It can cause painful swelling, purplish skin, blisters or cracking skin. Frostbite can have very serious consequences for the skin and can even lead to amputation. Someone with serious frostbite should not attempt to thaw out their skin, if there is a risk that it will freeze up again, which would be even more serious. It is best to get to a hospital as soon as possible.

The feet, hands, ears and face are the most suceptible to frostbite. It is best not to rub the affected area, but rather to apply heat (with your hands, for example). If the hands or feet are affected, it can be better to quicken your pace in order to increase the blood flow. Wear a wool hat, earwarmer and scarf to protect the ears and face.

■ Poison Ivy

Poison ivy is found in most natural regions of the northeastern United States. Unfortunately this harmful plant is difficult to recognize because it can adopt many contradictory characteristics: climbing or not, shiny or mat leaves, and differently coloured leaves depending on the season. All parts of the plant contain the offending oil (toxicodendrol) which is transmitted when it comes in contact with skin or clothing. The rash appears 24 to 48 hours after contact. The symptoms include painful itching, reddened skin, and bumps which become blisters. Someone who has come in contact with poison ivy should consult a physician.

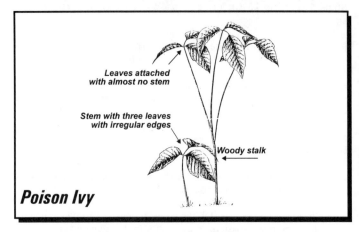

Three little tricks for identifying poison ivy:

- The leaves are in groups of threes.
- The stem of the centre leaf is longer than that of the other leaves.
- The middle vein of the leaf is off-centre.

■ Lyme Disease

Lyme disease is caused by disease-carrying ticks. There have been a number of reported cases in the United States. The disease is neither mortal, nor contagious, but if it is not treated it can lead to serious handicaps for the infected person. Skin lesions, fatigue, headaches, fever, joint and muscle pain and even problems related to the nervous system may appear a few days or weeks after being bitten. During the first weeks, antibiotic treatment has excellent results.

The tick is a small insect, the size of a pin head, which clings on to mammals and humans to suck their blood. The tick may stay attached for as many as 24 hours. If it is removed quickly (within a few hours), it can be neutralized and there is no danger. Note that some ticks are only carriers of Lyme disease. Do not squish the tick; remove it with a pair of tweezers by grasping the insect carefully close to the skin, making sure to extract the whole tick.

If you are hiking in an area where Lyme disease has been reported, take care to wear long pants and long-sleeved shirts, a hat and boots. At the end of the day, check all the parts of your body that were exposed during the day. Insecticides with DEET are effective at keeping these insects away. Call the local hiking club or an outdoor shop to see if these ticks are common in the area you plan to visit.

■ General Safety Tips

- Leave early (better to return at 2pm than 9pm).
- Give your complete itinerary to someone (friend, parent, spouse, etc.).
- When in a group, always wait for others at intersections.
- When in a group, take a head count often.
- Keep pace with the slowest person in the group.
- Stay on the trails.
- Do not underestimate the difficulty of the hike, or overestimate your abilities.
- Plan the hike at home, in advance.
- Always keep track of where you are on a map.
- Bring extra clothing, food and water.
- Bring a strong loud whistle.
- Use a topographic trail map and bring a compass (and know how to use it!).

Orientation

When hiking you will usually be following marked trails. Generally, hiking does not involve off-trail orienteering or require a compass. For most,

Types of markers

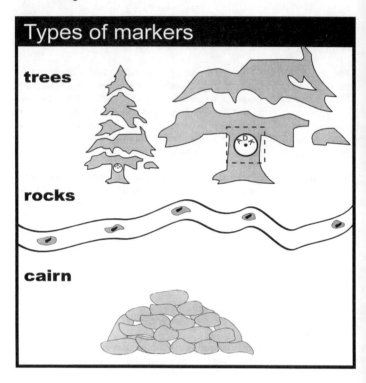

trees

rocks

cairn

the task of orientation requires little more than an understanding of the information provided by topographic trail maps. It is rare that you will have to use a compass on marked trails, except perhaps to identify a summit in the distance or to orient yourself in bad weather.

■ **Marked Trails**

Marked trails are usually identified by cairns, small signs or paint markings on trees or rocks. A cairn is a type of marker frequently used on bare mountain tops. It is essentially a pile of small boulders, about one metre high, indicating the trail to follow.

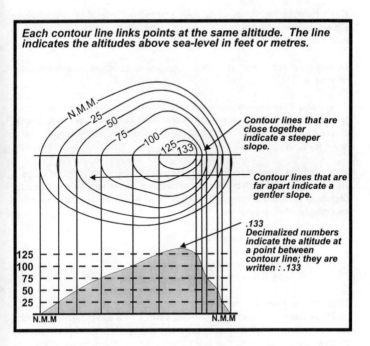

Each contour line links points at the same altitude. The line indicates the altitudes above sea-level in feet or metres.

Contour lines that are close together indicate a steeper slope.

Contour lines that are far apart indicate a gentler slope.

.133
Decimalized numbers indicate the altitude at a point between contour line; they are written : .133

Markers are spots of coloured paint on rocks or on the ground. The colour remains consistent for the duration of a given trail. The markers are spaced evenly so that it is easy to tell if you are on the right track. In case of doubt it is best to return to the last marker and pay special attention to the surroundings to make sure you are heading in the right direction.

■ **Topographic Maps**

Topographic maps (from the greek *topos*, place and *graphien*, to draw) are representations of a specific area of land drawn from aerial photographs. They show the relief of the land, as well as the distance and change in altitude between two points.

This information is crucial when hiking because the level of difficulty of a hike depends on the steepness, or slope, of the terrain much more than on the total distance covered.

A well-prepared hiker will have topographical maps which include existing trails.

Bring along a clear plastic case for maps to protect them from humidity and rain, (zip-lock freezer bags work well) or better yet buy them plasticized. Some maps are available made of a water-resistant, tear-proof material.

Topographical maps provide much more information than regular maps, and it is worth the effort to read through it all, especially the legend, usually located in the margin. The colours of the symbols follow certain topographical conventions:

> black = man-made objects
> blue = water (streams, rivers, lakes)
> green = vegetation
> brown = relief (irregularities of the terrain)

The contour lines are the lines on the map, usually drawn in brown, which indicate the mountains, hills and valleys. The space between each line represents a specific and constant change in altitude (in feet or metres), such that the farther apart the contour lines, the less steep the terrain, and vice versa (see illustration).

The cardinal points should be indicated on a topographical map. Unless otherwise stated north is at the top. There should also be a scale so that distances can be measured. When trying to measure a trail from the map it is easier and more accurate to use a piece of string than a ruler. Place the string along the curved trail line and then measure the length of string used.

■ Distance and Time

On a flat surface humans walk between 3.2 and 6.4 km/h. Going uphill this changes to between 1.6 and 3.2 km/h. There is an easy way to calculate the length of a particular hike: assume one hour for every 3 km covered and add an extra 1/2 hour for each 300 m of change in altitude. Take for example, a hike of 6 km with a change in altitude of

900 metres: 1 x 6/3 km = two hours, 1/2 x 900/300 m = one and a half hours, for a total of three and a half hours. This formula does not take into consideration all the variables that could affect your walking speed, such as:

- general physical fitness;
- how often you walk, your ability to pace yourself;
- the load you are carrying (backpack, footwear);
- the weather (rain, snow, heat, humidity);
- the quality of the trail (steepness, clear to follow);
- your familiarity with the particular trail (have you done it before);
- the varying ability of each hiker in a group (beginners, children, older people);
- the size of the group (frequent stops to rest, for water, for pictures).

■ Optional Trails

Once you have chosen to hike a specific trail, it is a good idea to check the map for other trails in the area that might serve as shortcuts or alternate routes in case of an accident to one of the hikers or bad weather conditions. These other trails might provide quicker access down the mountain in order to return to the departure spot and should be marked on your map with a grease pencil.

Climate and Temperature

The climate in the mountains is different from the climate at sea level. Up in the mountains weather changes are more frequent and less predictable. It is possible for a clear blue sky to darken all of a sudden and erupt into a fierce storm. Similarly, bad weather can disappear as quickly as it appeared.

There is generally more cloud cover at higher altitudes and therefore a greater chance of precipitation. The explanation for this phenomenon is that warm air from the valley is able to absorb more humidity than the cold air at the top of the mountain. Air is forced up by the mountain. The air cools and can no longer support the humidity — the results are cloud cover, heavy fog and precipitation in the form of snow or rain.

Once the air has passed the summit it descends again into the valley, warms up and is able to spread out once again. The sky clears up and it is a beautiful day in the valley.

The higher the altitude the lower the temperature, usually about 1°C per 180 m. The wind-chill factor can also lower the temperature drastically. In June 1945, for example, it was -22°C at the top of Mount Washington. The summit of Mount Washington is the site of the first mountain weather station, built in 1874.

The top of a mountain is that much closer to the sun. Solar radiation (the brightness of the sun) rises approximately 3% per 100 m increase in altitude. A good pair of sunglasses, an effective sun-screen lotion, and a hat are essential. A blanket of snow will intensify the reflection of ultraviolet rays. Also remember that in the mountains the air is much thinner and drier.

Wind Velocity km/h	Temperature in Celsius (°C)									
	10°	5°	-1°	-7°	-12°	-18°	-23°	-29°	-34°	-40°
	Temperature with windchill factor(°C)									
0km/h	10°	5°	-1°	-7°	-12°	-18°	-23°	-29°	-34°	-40°
8	9	3	-3	-9	-14	-20.5	-26	-32	-37.5	-44
16	5	-2	-9	-15	-23	-29.5	-36	-43	-50	-56.5
24	2	-6	-13	-20.5	-27.5	-37.5	-43	-50	-57.5	-64.5
32	0	-7.5	-15	-23	-32	-39	-47.5	-55	-63	-70.5
40	-1	-9	-18	-26	-34	-42	-51	-58.5	-66	-75
48	-2	-11	-19	-27.5	-36	-44.5	-52.5	-61	-69.5	-78
56	-3	-11.5	-20	-29	-37	-45	-55	-63	-72	-80
64	-3.5	-12	-21	-29.5	-38	-47.5	-56	-64.5	-73	-81.5

Normal winter conditions. Little danger provided appropriately dressed for weather.

Increased danger

Very dangerous

Freezing of exposed body parts.

■ Wind

In the mountains and on bare summits, wind is a significant factor. If there is a small breeze at the base of the mountain, you can be sure it is very windy at the summit. Not only does the wind make us work harder, it also has a dramatic effect on temperature. For example, if the temperature is 5°C and the wind speed is 50 km/h, the real temperature (the temperature we feel) will be -12°C. For this reason it is crucial to bring a warm sweater, an anorak, a tuque and gloves when you plan on heading uphill, even if it seems like a great day. The world record for wind velocity was set at the summit of Mount Washington: 370km/h in April 1934.

Temperature in Celsius (°C)

Relative humidity rate (%)	20	21	22	23	24	25	26	27	28	29	30	31	32	33	34	35
30								28	28	30	31	33	34	36	37	38
35					25	26	27	28	29	31	34	34	36	39	39	41
40				23	26	27	28	29	31	32	34	35	37	38	41	42
45		22	23	24	26	27	28	30	32	33	35	36	38	40	42	43
50	21	23	23	25	27	28	29	31	33	34	36	38	39	42	43	45
55	22	23	24	26	28	29	31	32	34	36	37	39	41	43	45	47
60	22	24	24	27	28	30	31	33	35	37	38	40	42	44	47	48
65	23	24	26	27	29	31	32	34	36	38	40	41	43	46	48	49
70	24	26	26	28	30	32	33	35	37	39	41	43	45	47	49	51
75	24	26	27	29	31	33	34	36	38	41	42	44	46	48	51	52
80	25	27	28	30	32	33	35	37	39	42	43	45	47	50	52	54
85	25	27	28	31	33	34	36	38	41	43	44	46	49	51	53	56
90	26	28	29	32	33	35	37	39	41	44	46	48	50	52	55	57
95	27	29	29	32	34	36	38	40	42	45	47	49	51	54	57	58
100	27	29	31	33	35	37	39	41	43	46	48	50	52	55	58	

moderate discomfort   extreme discomfort

■ Humidity

Just as wind can be a significant factor in cold weather, humidity can cause significant problems (in particular sunstroke) when it is hot. Remember that as of 26°C and 96% humidity, a hike will become more strenuous. Drinking a lot of water is essential.

The following table shows at which point a combined temperature and humidity become inadvisable. This is the humidex. You should be careful when the humidex rises above 40°C, pay attention to your body if you go hiking.

 ## Accommodations

The northeastern United States offers a wide selection of accommodations for hikers. We have listed seven of these, one or all of which are available in the regions covered.

Self-Serve and Free

- tent camping
- tarpaulin
- bivouac under the stars

Organized

- shelter
- lodge
- lean-to
- private campground

■ Tent Camping

Many areas, particularly in the Adirondacks, have designated areas where camping is permitted. It is usually possible to camp near lean-tos as well.

■ Tarpaulin

Camping under a tarpaulin shelter involves suspending the tarp between four trees. This allows the excitement of sleeping outside, while at the same time providing some protection from the elements. Tarpaulins are available in different sizes, can accommodate quite a few people, and are inexpensive. A rainy, windy night presents some problems since the rain is easily blown through the sides of the shelter. A tarpaulin also protects the campfire or campstove from rain, or it could serve as an eating area in the case of a long stretch of rainy days.

■ Bivouac Under the Stars

If you plan to sleep outdoors it is essential to bring some sort of ground sheet (that may double as a poncho) to keep your sleeping bag dry. Sleeping under the stars is another possibility. It may be necessary to bivouac, or tuck yourself into a cramped, uncomfortable spot in the event of bad weather. Some hikers bring along small bivouacs for sleeping bags (water-proof bags that fit over the sleeping bag).

A bivouac is ideal for those intrepid hikers who want a taste of the real outdoors. However sleeping in the open air present a few inconveniences and some precautions should be taken. Be sure to stay relatively close to a shelter, in case you need to return in the middle of the night, and choose your bivouac location carefully.

■ Shelters

Shelters are basically rustic cabins in which you are expected to be self-sufficient. In other words, you must provide your own food and warmth.

■ Lodges

These are more comfortable than shelters, but are still basically cabins. They are supervised and offer hot meals. Price vary and where possible reserving in advance is recommended.

■ Lean-Tos

A lean-to is a structure with three walls and a sloped roof. Even though one side is completely exposed, this structure still provides protection from wind and rain. Since reservations are impossible, it is important to arrange some other type of shelter (a tent) in case the lean-to is occupied (as is often the case on long weekends).

■ Private Camping

Camping in privately-run campgrounds close to the trails is another possibility, especially near Mount Washington and in Acadia National Park. You should look for loop trails since each night you will be returning to the same site. Private camping is often referred to as deluxe camping. It is ideal for families, older people or anyone who wants to be assured of a comfortable sleep. Keeping your baggage to a minimum becomes less important since your car is always nearby.

■ Choosing a Campsite

There are two reasons to avoid picking a mountain summit as a campground. First, the fragile mountain vegetation can be damaged by too much foot traffic. Second, temperatures are much lower on bare mountain summits which have no wooded areas to shield from high winds.

When contemplating a particular site, first ask yourself "Do I have permission to camp here?". You should find the answer before arriving at a site by contacting a tourist office (Adirondack Loj, Pinkham Notch, etc.) or by referring to a topographical map on which camping sites are usually indicated.

Night will invariably have begun to fall by the time the site has been chosen, with the tent, fire, water, etc. still to be taken care of. The best way to get things done quickly and efficiently is to divide the tasks.

It is important to set up camp, and dig your toilet, at least 50 m from the nearest water source to avoid contamination. Never wash dishes directly in the water source, even if you are using biodegradable soap, but rather in a container. Again, be sure to dump the waste-water at least 50 m away from any water source.

The same rule applies when your are cleaning yourself. Never do so in the water, even with biodegradable soap. Use a washcloth instead.

■ **Hotels, Motels, Inns ...**

For many of the areas we have also listed more conventional places to stay. These are better organized, offer more amenities, and are perhaps more in keeping with some hikers' tastes.

Customs

Canadian hikers travelling to the United States are entitled to a personal exemption upon their return to Canada. Each person is allowed to bring back goods valued up to a certain amount without having to pay any customs duties, GST or excise taxes. Of course, you can bring back as much merchandise as you want (with certain exceptions), but be prepared to pay taxes and duty on them.

If you are out of the country for less than 24 hours, you are ineligible for any personal exemptions.

If you are out of the country for 24 hours or longer, you can declare merchandise valued at up to a total of $20. There is no limit as to the number of declarations per year.

If you are out of the country for 48 hours or longer, you can declare merchandise valued at up to a total of $100. There is no limit to the number of declarations per year.

If you are out of the country for seven days or longer, you can declare merchandise valued at up to a total of $300. To do so, you must provide a written declaration, which you can only make once a year. For example, you cannot take two trips of a week or more and declare $150 of merchandise each time.

Maximum amounts of alcohol and tobacco products travellers are permitted to bring back with them:

● 200 cigarettes, 30 cigars, 400 grams of tobacco;
● 1.14 litres (40 ounces) of wine or spirits, or 24 355 ml (12 ounce) cans or bottles of beer. Beverages containing .5% alcohol per volume (wine, beer, coolers) are not included in this category.

Keep in mind that if a customs officer decides to make a more detailed inspection, it is your responsibility to open, unpack and repack your bags.

Information:

In Montreal: Canada Customs, 400 Place d'Youville, Montreal, H2C 2C2, ☎(514) 283-9900.

Hiking Etiquette Tips

Each hiker is one among millions. If the forest appears untouched, it is in part thanks to those who have passed before. As a hiker you should always make sure that the nature and beauty that you enjoy on a hike are preserved out of respect for hikers who will follow, and of course out of respect for nature itself. The environment is something that must be respected and protected.

This respect means sticking to the trail, since foot traffic can severely damage fragile mountain vegetation, even if there is snow on the ground. Do not walk on mountain bike or cross-country trails (unless the latter are multi-purpose). Respect private property signs.

Build fires only in designated areas and only with dead wood. Never cut firewood from living trees (live wood does not burn well anyway!). Whenever possible, prepare meals on a campstove, rather than a campfire. If a fire is absolutely necessary, make sure it is thoroughly extinguished when you are finished.

Do not take an axe or knife to a tree, and above all do not carve your sweetheart's initials in the bark. This will scar the bark and is a veritable wound for a tree. These gashes allow insects and fungi to penetrate the tree, thereby weakening its trunk and maybe even killing it.

Equally important is to camp only in designated areas, bringing all your garbage with you when you leave (aluminum and plastic do not completely burn). Do not throw anything into the water source (soap, urine, food, etc.), and do not feed the animals. Not only is this safer for you, it also shows respect for the animals.

Hikers should also be respectful of the group. Accept the pace of the slowest member, and the fatigue of others, so that everyone remains in good spirits. It is important to pull your own weight, pitch in as much as possible, and respect the needs of others for peace and quiet.

Often in a large group the most experienced member may be unofficially appointed the leader. This does not mean this person has the last word or may not welcome other ideas. Try to keep it democratic.

Pets

Domestic animals are permitted in most parks in the northeastern states. Nevertheless, it is a good idea to keep your animal on a leash, unless it is extremely well trained. Check with the park, organization or municipality that administers the region you will be visiting regarding the specific rules and regulations.

Organizing a Hike

A short one-day hike does not pose too many difficulties. It is important, however, not to overlook the aspect of security. In other words, bring along a first-aid kit, warm clothing, a flashlight, etc., just in case.

The key in hiking is good planning. The more time spent planning a hike, even just a one-day excursion, the more successful it will be. Take the time to find out what kind of plants, trees and birds to watch out for and once on the trail you'll be much more aware of your surroundings. It is also worth finding out what kind of cultural and historical activities, as well as other outdoor activities (swimming, canoeing, horseback riding, etc.) are possible on site or close by.

For longer hikes of two or more days with a group of people, preparing ahead of time is a must. At least one week in advance, organize a meeting with the entire group. This meeting will serve to acquaint everyone, to plan everything, to distribute the jobs, and, finally, to get everyone enthusiastic.

The following specifics should be worked out at this meeting:

- Introduction of each member (name, experience, expectations);
- Choice of itinerary (with topographical maps);
- Choice of menu (high energy, quick and easy to prepare);
- Organization of equipment for the group (tent, campstove, etc.);

- Each member's personal gear;
- Proper clothing for each member;
- Selection of a group leader (especially if most of the group is inexperienced);
- Trouble shooting for potential problems (weather, distances, etc.);
- Reservations, if necessary;
- Review of everyone's knowledge of orienteering, first aid, survival techniques, etc.;
- Delegating jobs (shopping for food and equipment);
- Organization of transportation;
- Review of everyone's state of health (those with allergies, heart conditions, diabetes, etc. should make the group aware of their conditions before the hike);
- Exchange phone numbers.

Bird-watching

Bird-watching and hiking go hand in hand. For experienced birders, hiking is the best mode of transportation for getting to prime birding sites. For hikers, curiosity leads them to bird-watch. As soon as an unknown species is spotted, there is a desire to identify it and understand it, and a birder is born.

Any season is a good one for bird-watching, though one season is particularly productive, and that's winter! Are there other things to see besides sparrows in the winter? Certainly! Winter is even considered the ideal season to start bird-watching. The fact that there are no leaves in the trees makes watching much easier. Furthermore, there are less species in the winter, and therefore it is easier to identify them.

Hiking is a great way to gain access to the birds' natural habitats. Depending on what species you are looking for, you might find yourself tramping over mountains, across fields and plains, along rivers, etc.

A beginner can easily observe more than 20 species, while an experienced birder will be able to spot up to 80. Among the species most commonly seen in winter in the northeastern United States are the blue jay, cardinal, hawfinch, chickadee, nuthatch, finch, longspur, redpoll, siskin (goldfinch) and waxwing.

A thoughtful hiker will bring along some sunflower seeds to attract chickadees, nuthatches, redpolls and others. You'll be astounded at how daring and curious these birds are, going so far as to eat right out of your hand. Besides a few sunflower seeds, bring along a pair of binoculars and birding book to help you identify what you see; a good one is *Peterson's Field Guide: All the Birds of Eastern and Central North America*, published by Houghton Mifflin.

Hiking and Children

There is no ideal age for hiking. Even children less than three years old can gain something... as long as there are willing arms to carry the little adventurer. Child-carrying backpacks are widely available in hiking and camping stores.

Beyond the age of three or four, children should have no problem walking the distance... but only if they want to! The concept of distance is inconsequential to a child; the prospects of discovery and adventure are what motivate them! As soon as a hike ceases to be fun, however, the little hiker will most probably also cease to move. It does not take much to break the spell, so it is a good idea not to venture too far from the car, or to be sure a strong back and shoulders are always available.

Older children and young adolescents like to pick and choose. At this age parents should include the children in some of the preparation and of course some of the responsibilities. Even better would be to sign up for an orienteering class with your child to develop their and your interest in hiking.

Adolescents may be hard pressed to leave the gang for a weekend in the great outdoors with Mom and Dad, so why not bring the whole gang along (within reason of course)! A longer hike complete with an overnight in tents or a shelter is a great way to show young adults how "cool" the outdoors and hiking really are!

Here are a few tips for a successful hike with children.

- Choose short and easy hikes with a high interest factor (such as self-guided or interpretational hikes).
- Hike before noon, leaving the afternoon open for the beach, etc.
- Protect children well from sun (sunhat, sunscreen), rain and mosquitoes.

- Make sure they drink water or juice constantly.
- Think of some games or songs for the hike (hide and seek, games with the compass, etc.).
- Leave extra space in the backpack for souvenirs.
- Follow the children's pace.
- Take short breaks.
- Prepare high-energy, tasty snacks.
- Encourage children to take photographs.
- Allow them to explore and climb (safely).
- Show interest in their discoveries (frogs, toads, worms, beetles, etc).
- Remember to bring along a younger child's favourite stuffed animal or toy.

■ Baby-carriers

Hiking, walking and speed-walking enthusiasts too often assume that the arrival of a baby means they can't be as active, yet nothing is farther from the truth. There are specialized stores that sell great, comfortable and functional baby-carriers of all kinds and for all activities.

Strollers

A recent innovation in the baby stroller that remains, for the most part, unknown is the three-wheel stroller, known as the "Baby Jogger". With its triangular design and big wheels that can tackle anything from mud to sand, grass and gravel it is versatile and easy to manoeuvre, it even has brakes. It is much more solid and performing than a conventional stroller and can handle just about any terrain, even a city sidewalk.

The "Baby Jogger" is made by the "Racing Strollers" company, it is ajustable and can handle up to 22 kg. Accessories like a roof to keep off the rain and sun, baskets and various wheel sizes are sold separately. They are quite expensive (about $400CAN), but also quite popular so you can resell it after a few months or years.

Backpack-style baby carriers

You'll need a backpack-style baby carrier for mountain hiking, where the terrain is steeper. Expect to pay between $100 and $200 CAN and make sure it has strong, wide and comfortable straps and lots of compartments. It should be stable so as not to unbalance the hiker. Some carriers are designed to placed on the ground either vertically or horizontally. A small roof to protect against the sun and rain can usually be added. Outdoor equipment stores sell and rent various types of baby carriers (around \$8 a day).

Equivalents

■ Length

1 cm	= 3.97 inch	1 inch	= 2.54 cm
1 m	= 3.28 feet	1 ft.	= 0.3 m
1 km	= 0.62 mile	1 mile	= 1.609 km

■ Mass

1 g	= 0.035 oz	1 oz	= 28.35 g
1 kg	= 2.2 lbs	1 lb	= 0.435 kg

■ Area

1 m2	= 10.76 ft2	1 ft2	= 0.09 m2
1 km2	= 0.39 mi2	1 mi2	= 2.6 km2
1 ha	= 2.47 acres	1 acre	= 0.4 hectare

■ Volume

1 l	= 0.22 gallon	1 gallon	= 4.54 l
1 l	= 0.26 US gallon	1 US gallon	= 3.79 l

■ Temperature

To convert:
°F to °C: subtract 32, divide by 9 and multiply by 5.
°C to °F: multiply by 9, divide by 5 and add 32.

EQUIPMENT

Shopping for equipment can be half the fun of preparing for a hike, and as with many other things you may find yourself tempted to follow the latest trends. In recent years equipment has become modernized. The clothing is more chic, the boots are lighter and the accessories are more sophisticated. This trend has certainly made hiking more visually attractive. More importantly, though, it has made hiking more comfortable.

Of course, innovation automatically costs more, and hiking is no exception. For many this financial obstacle will be no obstacle at all, but for others such an investment is hard to justify. Most hikers start with basic equipment, and find it is no hindrance to their enjoyment of hiking. As long as you are comfortable and safe you can easily hike the same trail as the hiker who is decked out in top-of-the-line gear.

Hiking is not for everyone, so before you spend a fortune on costly equipment take a few test runs. There are places in the major centres where you can rent equipment. This will help you decide what gear you need and save you money in the long run.

The small snags encountered on your first hikes will determine what equipment is best suited to your needs, and help you distinguish between what is essential, what is superfluous, and what is useful but can wait.

The Essentials

Here are some descriptions of what is available:

■ The Backpack

Up until a couple of years ago there were two types of backpacks on the market: external frame packs and internal frame packs. The former have virtually disappeared from the market, mainly as a result of improvements in the construction of internal frame packs, which are much lighter and easier to adjust to the body.

A good backpack should have the following:

- A well-padded waist belt;
- compression straps along the side of the bag to decrease the volume of the bag and to keep the weight of the bag close to the body;
- the possibility of adjusting the length of the bag between the belt and the shoulder straps to fit the back;
- a clasp across the chest that joins the shoulder straps
- compartments on the outside of the bag;
- about 60 to 80 L of volume (the larger the bag, the greater the temptation to fill it);
- eyes and straps to which items may be attached;

When packing, always start with the sleeping bag at the bottom. Next add things you will not need through the course of the day, such as the campstove and clothing for the evening and night. Finally, on top, put the clothing and essentials you will need as you hike. It is important to put the heaviest gear, which is usually the food, two thirds of the way down into the bag. The mattress can be attached between the bag and the pocket on top, strapped to the side, or if the backpack is big enough, placed inside. In this case roll the mattress up and place the equipment in the middle of it.

Attaching things to the outside of your backpack is generally not a good idea, as they disrupt your balance and can get caught on branches. A water bottle is the only thing that should go on the outside of the bag.

For one day hikes a small backpack (about 30 L) is sufficient. It should be big enough to carry a water bottle, camera, first-aid kit, maps, compass, food for the day and extra clothing. Check that it is solid, especially the shoulder straps.

■ The Sleeping Bag

As with for clothing, the insulating ability of the sleeping bag depends on the thickness of the insulation. The thicker the bag, the warmer it will be. At the same time, however, bags of varying weights may offer the same insulation value. For example a down-filled bag is lighter than a bag insulated with "Polarguard". However, down-filled bags lose their insulation value when wet and take a long time to dry. Also in a humid climate, down presents a problem, unless the shell of the bag is made of a breathable fabric (like "Gore-Tex"). It is therefore a better idea to buy a bag insulated with synthetic materials that dry faster and are more reliable in wet weather, even though it may be heavier and cost more.

Mummy bags are warmer because they eliminate the extra space between your body and the bag, space which eventually fills with cold air. There are different sizes of sleeping bags so do not hesitate to try them on in the store. A bag with a temperature rating of -5°C is sufficient for summer (-12°C for spring and fall).

It is important to check that the zipper is protected by a flap which prevents cold air from blowing into the bag. If the sleeping bag takes up too much room in the backpack, use straps to compress it and decrease its volume.

Proper care of your sleeping bag will ensure that the insulation lasts. To avoid deterioration of the insulation do not store the sleeping bag rolled up or stuffed into its sack. Take it out after each trip and keep it on a hanger.

These are the synthetic insulations available today: "Polarguard", "Hollofil" and "Quallofil". For the same weight "Quallofil" provides the most warmth. "Polarguard HV" which is light and compresses well, is a popular choice these days.

■ The Insulating Mattress

These mattresses are essential if you want to take full advantage of the insulating capability of your sleeping bag. On a long hike it is impossible to carry a large, heavy, inflatable air mattress. Small, closed-cell foam mattresses are therefore ideal. They are lightweight, waterproof, and easily attached to the exterior of the pack. They are available in three thicknesses, 0.75 cm, 1 cm, 1.5 cm. Also available are small inflatable air mattresses that insulate well and are very comfortable, but expensive.

An insulating mattress, or simple foam mattress, is ideal for comfortable rest stops (at lookout points, lunch, rest). There is not always a nice piece of grass on which to stretch out in the middle of a hike, and since the ground is often wet, it is a good idea to get in the habit of keeping a mattress handy. Relatively inexpensive (about $15), a foam mattress can easily accommodate two people. Or you may opt for a self-inflating mattress (Therm-A-Rest from $60 to $90), which insulates well and is very comfortable, but also quite expensive.

An insulating mattress can be placed between the backpack and the upper pocket, attached to the side of the bag, or if the backpack is big then inside the bag in a cylinder shape around the sides of the bag. All the other equipment would thus go inside the mattress.

■ The Tent

To be effective a tent must keep out wind, rain, and bugs. It also has to be quick and easy to set up, and big enough to offer basic comfort. If it has no pegs you can move it around after it is assembled.

Arched frame poles joined by elastic make it easier to mount the tent. In order to maximize space you may want to add a vestibule where bags and gear can be kept. Finally, the tent should be light and compact: about 3 kg for 2 people, and approximately 3.5 kg for 3 people. A good tent will have a double roof, or fly, of waterproof nylon with waterproof seams. The fly should rest far enough above the tent so as not to touch it. It should also come far enough down the sides of the tent to properly protect it from wind. The screen of the tent must be fireproof and large enough to provide sufficient ventilation. Expect to spend around $300 for a good three-season tent.

■ The Campstove

The most important considerations here are efficiency and weight. Efficiency means the amount of time it takes to boil a litre of water. Stoves that use naphthalene are generally more efficient, but they require more maintenance and are often difficult to light in cold weather.

Alcohol burning stoves are more practical. They are easy to light, work in any temperature, and require little maintenance. Their main drawback is the difficulty of adjusting the flame. Butane stoves are also practical, but, like the naphtha-fuelled type, are inefficient in cold weather. There are also stoves that work with various different fuels (naphtha, kerosene, alcohol, unleaded gasoline, etc.) Which are good for travelling in foreign countries. "MSR" brand stoves are popular with hikers.

■ The Mess Kit

Many portable stoves come complete with a mess kit. If this is not the case you will need to buy pots, but make sure they don't take up half your bag. Usually a kit comes with a multi-purpose handle for moving hot pots, and a set of dishes and cups. It should include a 1.7 l to 2 l pot and be made of stainless steel. The top should also serve as a frying pan. The dishes and cups should be plastic so that food does not cool too quickly. Large plastic mugs are available that insulate and have tops. They are inexpensive and keep things warm longer. A pocketknife, fork, spoon and a dish towel will complete your travelling kitchen.

■ The Water Bottle

A one litre water bottle with a large neck is ideal. It is easy to fill without getting your hands wet, and the opening will not freeze as quickly in cold weather. Look for the "Nalgene" brand, they are light, strong (polycarbonate Lexan), watertight and don't give a plastic taste to water.

Avoid using leather gourds. They give a foul taste to the water and will eventually soak through to your backpack. To avoid frozen water, place the bottle in your backpack so that it is against your back. Your body heat will keep the water liquid. Insulated bottle-carriers are available.

■ The Compass

A compass is not essential when you are following marked trails. You may want to bring one along in case of emergency or just for fun. Since hiking is not orienteering, you do not need a hi-tech model. A simple "Sylva" compass ($10 to $15) will do the job. A compass will allow you to orient your map properly in the absence of any visible landmarks. Once at the summit it will also allow you to identify other mountains in the distance.

It is a good idea to have some information on how to use a compass or to follow a course (check with outdoor club or school). Otherwise ask an experienced friend to give you some pointers before heading out.

■ The Flashlight

The ideal flashlight is one that can be worn on the head like a miner's lamp (Petzl, about $35). It leaves both hands free to do other things like walking, finding trail markers, looking at a map or guide, etc. If ever a hiker is caught out after dark, a lamp like this can be a life-saver, it will light up to a distance of 30 m (or 100 m with a halogen bulb).

■ The Pocketknife

You will find a million uses for a folding pocketknife, for meals, repairs and cutting laces or branches. Two types are particularly popular with hikers: the Opinel ($10 to $20) and the Swiss Army Knife ($25 to $100 +).

■ The Repair Kit

The repair kit must be versatile. With few materials you should be able to repair big items, at least temporarily. The kit should contain supplies for the stove, some copper wire, a small sewing kit, a small pair of pliers, and a pair of shoelaces.

■ Accessories

Several little accessories can make your hike more enjoyable and safer. Among these, waterproof matches, some string, a whistle, sunglasses, sunscreen, lip balm, insect repellent, a walking stick plus various plant and wildlife identification guides are all useful. Remember that all of these items are inexpensive ($10 to $20) and make great gifts!

■ Footwear

Footwear is the most important piece of equipment in hiking. It is the first thing that beginner hikers should purchase. Much has changed since the days when boots were heavy and rigid and you had to suffer for months before breaking them in. Specialized stores offer a wide selection of hiking footwear for all tastes and budgets.

Depending on the type of hiking there are three types of footwear.

Walking shoes are useful for light hiking trips of one day on groomed trails without steep inclines. A whole new line of all-terrain shoes have hit the stores recently. They are lightweight, shock absorbent, sturdy, usually made of leather and are a good buy for those who don't plan on tackling any high mountains or long hikes. Expect to pay about $100.

Light hiking boots will allow you to conquer some more imposing peaks on one-day hikes by providing more ankle support than walking shoes do. They are adequate for hikes of more than one day, but your ankles will begin to feel it, especially on a rough trail toting a backpack weighing a few kilos. Usually a combination of leather and nylon, these boots are a good choice for hikers on a budget. Expect to pay $100.

Hiking boots are useful for all hikes. They are higher and stronger than the other two types and therefore sufficient for mountain hiking and for hiking on rough, uneven trails. Ankle support is excellent. Made of leather, these boots offer comfort, support, stability, traction, shock absorption and durability. They need to be cleaned and protected regularly (non-silicone beeswax). Expect to pay between $150 and $200.

Semi-rigid and rigid hiking boots ($200 to $300) are also available for long expeditions on steep terrain (alpine conditions).

When trying on boots in the store remember the following advice:

- Choose the right socks depending on the kind of hiking you'll be doing (city walking, short hike, long hike, polypropylene, wool, etc.) and wear them when you try the boots on;
- Don't shop the day after a late night out;
- Go to a specialized store;
- Make sure you have enough time to make the right choice;
- Make sure to try on both boots, most people have one foot bigger than the other;
- Make sure there is no excess pressure on the top of the foot;
- Before tying up the laces, slide your foot to the front of the boot, you should be able to get a finger between your heel and the back of the boot (remember your feet will swell while hiking);
- Walk around with the shoes on for at least 10 minutes in order to get a genuine idea of how they fit;
- make sure your heel stays in place;
- "Gore-Tex"-lined boots are waterproof to a point; seams can leak. If your feet sweat a lot, these are not best buy;
- A pair of gaiters over the boots will keep your feet dryer for longer and will keep out little pebbles and snow on rough terrain;
- Make sure you can return or exchange the boots, and once at home walk around indoors with them for a few hours to ensure they fit properly;
- Maintaining your boots is essential. After a hike, clean off any mud or snow, and dry them out. Do not place them too close to a heat source. Stuff them with newspaper to help them keep their shape. Finally, treat boots with an appropriate product to protect them and waterproof them.

Clothing

As much as you need to cover yourself up at night you should also pay close attention to what you wear during the day, in order to maintain the ideal body temperature (37°C). What you wear in all types of weather and at all times of the day is crucial. Clothing insulates and protects the body from the surrounding air; it protects you from the heat and from the cold.

Water is a good heat conductor. It is therefore important to wear clothes that breathe, meaning that they keep you warm while at the same time allowing perspiration to evaporate. In the case of anoraks (Gore-Tex or otherwise), you want something that lets the sweat out and keeps the rain from coming in.

Fleece or "synchilla" are very useful in this respect. They insulate well and dry more quickly than wool. Layering is the best way to dress when hiking. You can take off or add layers as your body warms and cools, without too drastic a change.

Never wait until you start sweating before removing a layer. Rather, take it off as soon as you begin to feel warm. A ski jacket is not a good idea because you will be too warm with it on and too cold without it.

Layers for the upper body should consist of the following:

- Undershirt that breathes (polypropylene, etc.);
- Fleece or wool sweater;
- Anorak (if it is not made of "Gore-Tex" or of similar fabric, it is better to have an anorak that breathes and a raincoat);
- Tuque;
- Mittens or gloves.

Layers for the lower body consist of:

- Long underwear that breathes (polypropylene, etc.);
- Lightweight, loose-fitting pants;
- Waterproof or "Gore-Tex" pants;
- Two pairs of socks, to avoid friction (one pair of polypropylene or cotton socks next to your skin and another wool pair);
- Gaiters.

Gaiters keep mud, rocks, snow and water from getting into boots. They also help to keep feet warm and to protect socks and pants from soiling. On long hikes, in rainy, muddy weather gaiters ($20 to $60) are indispensable.

■ Layering

The layering system usually involves three types of clothing. In cold weather, or on bare windy summits, however, it is not unheard of for a hiker to wear five or six layers. Each of these several layers corresponds to these three types of clothing which permit optimal comfort when exercising in the outdoors.

First layer

The first layer of clothing is underwear (tops and bottoms). It keep the body dry by wicking moisture away from the body. The loss of heat is 32 times greater if the skin surface is humid, staying dry is therefore essential. In recent years the most effective long underwear has been made of treated polyester (100%). Thin and form-fitting, they are also very soft to the touch.

Note that there are four or five different thicknesses in underwear. Which one you choose will depend on the season, where you are visiting, what activity you are practising and whether you get a chill easily.

Second layer

The second layer is meant to conserve the body heat while at the same time allowing the humidity wicked away by the first layer to pass. In recent years, "synchilla" fabric has become the most popular choice for this layer. Like underwear, synchilla is made of 100% polyester. Though the same fibres are used, the name varies considerably depending on the manufacturer.

There are also different thicknesses of synchilla (usually three), the thinnest is often similar to the thickest underwear. Besides being quick-drying, synchilla is very comfortable. It is very warm in cold weather and also wearable in warm weather, whereas a wool sweater is unbearable in hot weather.

Watch out for inexpensive imitation "synchilla" sweaters, that are nothing more than brushed felt which wears out quickly and does not conserve body heat. If you haven't got a synchilla, wear a wool sweater (not cotton), wool has the distinct advantage of keeping you warm, even when wet.

Third layer

The third layer protects the body from the elements, wind, rain and snow. Parkas, jackets and nylon pants do this. A longer parka may simply act as a windbreaker, a raincoat, or both at once.

A jacket is ideal when you are doing a more demanding activity (speed walking, bicycling, cross-country skiing, etc.) in warmer weather. It is inexpensive but not waterproof. A raincoat is great for bad weather. Also inexpensive, it will protect you from rain and snow, but becomes a veritable sauna with the least bit of exertion.

The best option for hiking, as well as for most outdoor activities, is the parka (with or without pants), which is waterproof but also breathable. Gore-Tex, a membrane that is sewn into clothing to make it waterproof and breathable, is a favourite with hikers. The durability and effectiveness of this product has been continuously improved upon recently. Other products that are applied as coatings also offer an excellent protection against the elements and are also breathable (Entrant, Sympatec, Triple Point, Dermoflex, etc.).

These kinds of parkas or jackets are quite expensive ($200 to $500) but offer excellent year-round protection. Watch for the thickness (number of layers), the lining, the cut (with respect to your waist), the wrists (adjustable) and above all ventilation (zipper under the arms).

■ Day Clothing

When hiking, there are two types of clothing, that worn during the day and that worn at night. Day clothing is worn while actually hiking. Within this category, there is cold weather and warm weather clothing.

Cold Weather

According to McArdle and Katch in *Exercise Physiology*, the weave of clothing fibres trap warm air against the body and therefore insulate from the cold. Since clothing and air are poor conductors of heat, they form a barrier against heat loss. The more air that is trapped against the skin, the better insulated it will be. This is why several layers of thinner clothing, or clothes lined with fur or synthetic fibres (made up of several layers of trapped air), provide better insulation than just one heavy winter jacket.

As soon as you begin to get chilled the first thing to add is a tuque or some sort of hat, since your body loses 30% to 40% of its heat through the head.

Dry clothes should be your priority in cold weather, since clothing dampened by rain or sweat loses 90% of its insulating capability. If you do not have an anorak to protect you from the rain ("Gore-Tex", "Dermoflex", etc.), you should bring a raincoat as well as a cotton or nylon windbreaker. Never forget to bring a tuque and gloves or mittens since evenings and mornings can be quite chilly at higher altitudes.

During the hike you will probably wear an anorak over your undershirt, whether warm or cool, keeping the fleece or wool sweater for rest stops, meals, and evenings.

It is not a good idea to wear jeans. Generally they are too tight, too heavy and take too long to dry. Cotton pants (or jogging pants), cotton/nylon pants, or corduroy pants, are better ideas. The warmest fabrics (in decreasing order) are wool, cotton, flannel and nylon.

Warm Weather

Most hikers find the heat more difficult to bear than the cold. This explains why there are fewer hikers on the trails of the northeastern United States during the month of July than in the fall.

Dressing for warm weather is not as easy as it would seem. Wearing shorts may be the most comfortable option, until you wander into low-lying brush and your legs get scratched. Ultra-light nylon pants are better.

Warm weather clothing must be ample to allow air to circulate between the fabric and your skin and to allow perspiration to evaporate. Colour is also important. Dark colours absorb more light and therefore more heat than light colours. Even with loose light-coloured clothing, your body will only cool down when your clothes become wet and the cooling evaporation can occur. According to W.D. McArdle, a physiology professor at the University of New York, putting on a new dry shirt in hot weather goes against the phenomenon of thermoregulation. He proposes that the loss of heat due to evaporation, which creates a cooling sensation, will only happen when your clothing is completely wet. Therefore to beat the heat it is better to keep your wet shirt on than to change it for a dry one, which would only put off the eventual cooling evaporation of your body's sweat.

■ **Night Clothing**

Dressing for nighttime is essentially the same as dressing for cold weather. It is especially important to dress warmly at night (even in the summer) because the body has a tendency to cool down after a long day of exercising. Also in the mountains the drop in temperature after sundown is much more significant. During the spring and fall most hikers find they need a down vest and slippers to sleep in.

Keeping warm at night is a priority. Without a good night sleep you risk wasting the morning in bed, or spending the day overtired.

What you actually wear while sleeping will depend on your sleeping bag. If you have a good bag, that is a warm one, you could sleep naked. If your bag's insulating ability is not high then it is best to get dressed for bed a while before actually going to bed. Leave your long underwear on (top and bottom) to maintain your body's warmth. A fleece or wool sweater may be needed in really cold weather, and of course remember to wear a tuque since most of your body heat escapes through your head.

What to Bring

■ **One-Day Hikes**

Clothing

- hiking boots
- long underwear
- t-shirt
- extra pair of socks
- parka or jacket
- synchilla or wool sweater
- pants
- wind-resistant pants
- gaiters
- mitts or gloves
- tuque

Accessories

- backpack
- insulating mattress
- sunglasses
- toilet paper
- binoculars
- camera
- small flashlight
- knife
- water bottle
- matches
- string
- whistle
- plastic bag
- insect repellent
- sunscreen

- UV lip balm
- map of the area
- guidebooks (hiking, flora, fauna)
- compass
- notebook and pencil

First Aid Kit

- Compeed
- moleskin
- antibiotic ointment
- pain reliever (Tylenol, aspirin)

- elastic bandage (Ace)
- compressor bandage
- 3 sterile plastic bandages
- plastic bandages
- small scissors
- tweezers
- pins, safety pins and razor blades
- matches
- sterile gauze
- glucose tablets
- sanitary napkins
- alcohol swabs

■ Long Hikes

Clothing

- windbreaker
- wool sweater
- two t-shirts
- two sets of polypropylene underwear
- nylon pants
- wind-resistant pants
- 4 pairs of socks (cotton and wool or polypropylene)
- small gloves
- gaiters
- tuque
- hiking boots

Camping Equipment

- tent
- sleeping bag
- ground sheet
- backpack

Kitchen Equipment

- campstove
- fuel
- mess kit
- pocketknife, forks, spoons
- small plastic plates
- plastic cups
- dish rag
- ecological steel wool

First-Aid Kit

- one pair of scissors
- 3 sterile plastic bandages
- butterfly bandages
- antibiotic ointment
- moleskin
- safety pin, needle, razor blade
- matches

- pain reliever (Tylenol, aspirin)
- sterile gauze
- glucose tablets
- sanitary napkins
- alcohol swabs
- UV lip balm

Ready-made first aid kits can also be purchased in pharmacies and outdoor shops.

Equipment Rental

Instead of purchasing all of the equipment necessary for long hikes, which can be quite costly, try renting out a few items (from camping stores, outing clubs, universities or colleges). Campstoves, mess-kits, backpacks, sleeping bags, saws, etc, can all be rented at reasonable prices, giving you the opportunity to decide what best suits your needs when it comes time to buy. You will also determine if you are the type of hiker who prefers to carry their life on their back for a few days, or perhaps the comforts of a well-stocked lodge are more your style!

Repairs

Early spring is the best time to take an inventory of your equipment. You might find there are several little repairs to make: a broken zipper, a torn jacket, sleeves that are too long or too short, pants to take in, uncomfortable or broken backpack straps or sleeping bags and tents that need to be overhauled.

If your camping or hiking equipment breaks, before replacing it consider repairing it. The same thing goes for your hiking boots.

Maps

The maps in this guide will help you locate the specific area for each hike. However, **they are not topographical maps** and serve only to situate you in relation to nearby towns and roads.

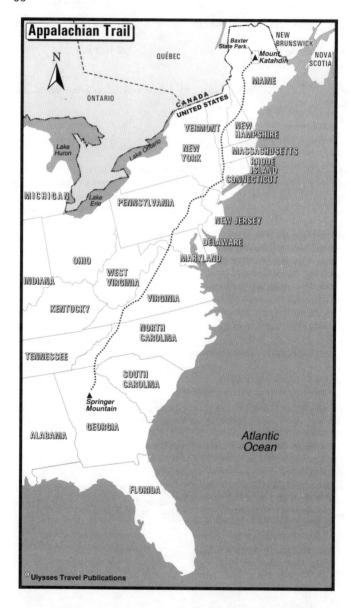

CLASSIFICATION OF HIKES

The hikes suggested are organized according to level of difficulty: easy, difficult or very difficult. The levels are represented in the guide by the following symbol:

(easy):	short hike with little change in altitude.
(difficult):	long hike with little change in altitude **OR** short hike with significant change in altitude.
(very difficult):	long hike with significant change in altitude **OR** extremely long hike **OR** long hike with very large change in altitude.

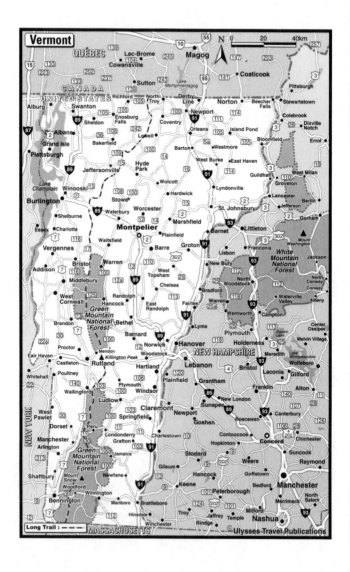

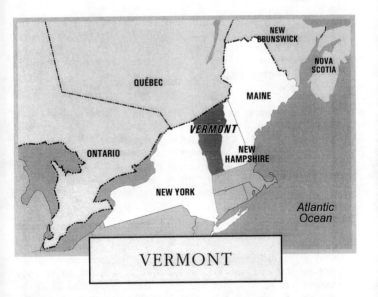

VERMONT

Vermont's nickname, the Green Mountain State is truly deserved. Everywhere you look, there are magnificent valleys and majestic mountains abounding in greenery. Flamboyant in some places and soothing in others, the omnipresent green is boken here and there by a little blue house, a red barn or a wooden church all in white.

Supposedly, this part of the country was named Vermont (*Vert Mont* is French for "green mountain") by Reverend Samuel Peters in 1763. After riding his horse to the top of Killington Peak (1,293 m), the second highest mountain in the state, Peters decided that the name suited this immense landscape perfectly. Local residents have adopted the English translation, so that the words "Green Mountain" figure in the name of everything from hiking clubs, restaurants and antique shops to syrup and coffee.

Local residents' pride in their state is evident throughout Vermont. Many Americans move here to live in harmony with both nature and their fellow man. Life in Vermont is peaceful, and seems to go by at a gentler pace than in the neighbouring states. Furthermore, the landscape remains unaffected by consumer society, since roadside billboards are prohibited.

Vermont is a tiny state, it is only 240 km long and less than 150 km wide at its largest point (in the north). With only 500,000 inhabitants, it is the third smallest state in the country in terms of population. Its capital, Montpelier, has only 8,000 residents. The largest city in the state is Burlington (pop. 40,000), the second largest, Rutland (pop. 20,000).

There are mountains all over Vermont, and 75% of its territory is covered by forests. Of the six New England states, it is the only one with no access to the Atlantic Ocean. People say that if you want to insult a Vermonter, ask him which road leads to the sea! The Green Mountains stretch all the way down the state, from Quebec in the north to Massachusetts in the south. This mountain range is crisscrossed by a unique hiking trail, the celebrated Long Trail.

The Long Trail

The Long Trail (LT) covers a distance of 437 km through the Green Mountains. Created between 1910 and 1930, it is the oldest "long distance" trail in the United States and leads to the tops of all the loftiest mountains in Vermont: Mansfield (1,339 m; highest point in the state), Killington (1.293 m), Camel's Hump (1,244 m), Ellen (1,244 m), Abraham (1,221 m), etc. Some 282 km of secondary trails branch off from the main trail, providing different routes up the mountains.

There are a several campgrounds along the Long Trail, as well as many shelters. At the major shelters, usually located near the highest summits, there is a caretaker who can provide you with information on the trail, its historical background and the fragile vegetation you'll encounter along the way, especially on the mountain tops. An overnight stay costs $4.

In spring, particularly from March to the end of May, hikers are strongly urged to avoid those parts of trails leading across the higher mountaintops, since doing so can seriously damage the wet soil. The entire Mount Mansfield-Camel's Hump region is closed during this period.

In the southern part of the state, the Long Trail overlaps with the Appalachian Trail (AT) for 160 km, from Route 4 (Shelburne Pass) to the Massachusetts border.

To learn more about the Long Trail, pick up a copy of the *Long Trail Guide* (see "Recommended Reading", p 230). The first edition of this excellent guide, published by the celebrated Green Mountain Club (GMC), was put out in 1917! 1996 marks its 24th edition. Any number of day-long hikes can be enjoyed on the Long Trail, which is divided into 12 sections. Of course, you can also cover the entire distance, if you're up for a little stroll through the woods!

The Green Mountain Club

The Green Mountain Club (GMC) was founded the year the Long Trail was created, in 1910, and now has some 6,500 members. In addition to taking care of the trail, the club provides information on hiking in Vermont. Numerous guides, books, maps and brochures bear the GMC stamp.

The offices of the Green Mountain Club are located on Route 100, in Waterbury Center, between the villages of Stowe and Waterbury. For all information on hiking in Vermont, telephone, write or stop by the Hiker Center (open every day from 9am to 5pm). The club even has a list of members who can drive you to the starting point of a hike, which can be very useful when the trail in question does not form a loop.

Green Mountain Club: Route 100, R.R. 1, Box 650, Waterbury Center, Vermont 05677, ☎ (802) 244-7037.

Mount Mansfield Region

Mount Mansfield (1,340 m) is Vermont's highest peak, 95 m higher than the Camel's Hump. The controversy over which peak was highest lasted for many years and was only settled one morning by an ingenious hunter who arose early and climbed Mount Mansfield with his rifle and a lead ball-bearing. At the summit, he placed the lead in the barrel of his rifle, set his sights on the peak of Camel's Hump, and as the lead rolled out of the rifle, Mount Mansfield was proven to be the highest.

Before the arrival of the colonists, the Abenaki Indians called this peak "Moze-o-de-be-wadso", which means "moose-head". The white man was reminded of a different beast's head, however, and named it Mansfield in his own image. Each part of the mountain was subsequently named for a different part of the human face: nose, chin, upper and lower lips, forehead and Adam's apple. Once on the small road that leads to Underhill State Park, you should be able to distinguish (with a little imagination) the various features of a man's head, or maybe you'll decide the natives were closer to the mark.

The popularity of the Green Mountains and Mount Mansfield with the white colonists began more than 100 years ago. People came from the larger urban centres of New England and scaled the mountains on foot, on horseback, and in cars. They came for the sunrises and the sunsets. The main peaks were equipped with small rustic houses called "summit houses". Most of these were closed around the turn of the century, except the one on Mount Mansfield which remained open until 1960.

Covering the crest of Mount Mansfield is the largest zone of arctic and alpine vegetation in Vermont, left over from the ice age. This phenomenon in itself constitutes an ecological gold mine. With the retreat of the last glaciers, small arctic plants began to grow. For the most part they disappeared with the slow warming of the earth, except on three Vermont summits, Mount Mansfield, Camel's Hump (1,244 m) and Mount Abraham (1,221 m).

The weather conditions on these summits are similar to those of arctic regions. The layer of unfrozen earth is not very deep, winds are often violently strong, temperatures are colder and the growing season is shorter. These conditions limit the vegetation to small clusters of arctic growth, and few varieties survive along the paths. Around 40,000 people hike the trails of Mount Mansfield every year. This kind of traffic puts a strain on the survival of these plants. To avoid complete destruction of this fragile balance a few guidelines should be followed:

- Walk only on marked trails, and if possible only on rock surfaces;
- Do not pick any wild plants (most of the plant life is actually protected by law);
- No campfires above 760 m.

 Finding Your Way Around

The closest major highway to Mount Mansfield is Interstate 89 in the vicinity of northern Vermont, close to the Canadian border. Coming from the north, at the town of North Fairfax on Interstate 89, follow Route 104 South to Cambridge. From there your route depends on the

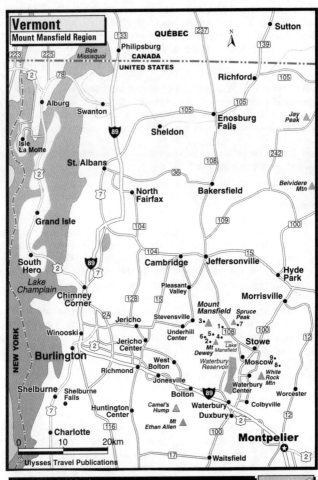

Vermont
Mount Mansfield Region

QUÉBEC
Philipsburg
CANADA
UNITED STATES
Sutton
Richford
Baie Missisquoi
Alburg
Swanton
Sheldon
Enosburg Falls
Jay Peak
Isle La Motte
St. Albans
North Fairfax
Bakersfield
Belvidere Mtn
Grand Isle
South Hero
Cambridge
Jeffersonville
Hyde Park
Lake Champlain
Chimney Corner
Pleasant Valley
Mount Mansfield
Spruce Peak
Morrisville
Jericho
Stevensville
Underhill Center
Winooski
Jericho Center
Burlington
West Bolton
Stowe
Moscow
Mt Dewey
Lake Mansfield
White Rock Mtn
Richmond
Jonesville
Waterbury Reservoir
Waterbury Center
Shelburne
Shelburne Falls
Bolton
Waterbury
Colbyville
Worcester
NEW YORK
Huntington Center
Camel's Hump
Duxbury
Charlotte
Mt Ethan Allen
Montpelier
Waitsfield
0 10 20km
© Ulysses Travel Publications

Mount Mansfield Region

1. Haselton Trail
2. Sunset Ridge
   Laura Cowles
   Halfway House
   Loop from Underhill State
   Camping Area
3. Butler Lodge
   Maple Ridge Trail
   Long Trail
4. Long Trail
5. Subway
   Tundra Trail
6. Hell Brook Trail
7. Elephant's Head Trail
8. Mount Hunger
9. Stowe Pinnacle Mountain

trail you plan to hike. To get to Underhill State Park, take Pleasant Valley Road which is on the left immediately after the Cambridge General Store. Coming from the south, exit off Interstate 89 just north of Burlington onto Route 15 and continue along it to Jeffersonville, then take Route 104 for the above-mentioned starting points.

If your hike is on the other face of Mount Mansfield continue along to Jeffersonville via Route 15. At Jeffersonville take Route 108 South to Smuggler's Notch. If you decide to drive the notch make sure your brakes are in good shape as the road is very steep and very narrow.

Buses cannot take this road because the curves are too sharp, they will have to go by Waterbury and Stowe.

■ Parking

- Underhill State Camping Area: from Pleasant Valley Road turn left after the sign for the campsite. The sign is not very visible and the road is steep, so drive slowly to avoid missing it. It is 6 km along the partially paved road to the campsite. Parking is free, but there is a $1.50 fee to get into the park.

- Stevensville: continue along Pleasant Valley Road and take the small road to the left before reaching Underhill Center. Leave your car by the side of the road where the road ends and the trails begin.

- Smuggler's Notch: at the top of the notch there is a small parking area with about ten parking spots, this area provides access to the trails on the east side.

- Smuggler's Notch State Camping Area: take Route 108 from Stowe to the Stowe Ski Center. There are three parking areas: the Ski Center's lot, the Camping Area lot to the right, and the Spruce Peak Ski Area lot, which is far from the trails.

? Practical Information

■ **Camping Stores**

Umiak Outdoor Outfitters
849 South Main
Stowe
☎ (802) 253-2317

Climb High
1861 Shelburne Rd
Shelburne (south of Burlington)
(☎ 802-985-5055)

■ **Tourist Information**

Stowe Area Association
☎ 1-800-24-STOWE

 Exploring

Follow the motorized-vehicle-free Stowe Recreation Path by foot, bike, or in-line skates... and do so in complete peace! The path starts in Stowe and is 8,5 km long (one-way).

The **Shelburne Museum** ☎ (802) 985-3344, 3346: Located south of Burlington, this historical museum includes 40 buildings which recount the bygone days of life in New England.

Take a stroll along the 192-km-long shores of Lake Champlain, or on Grande Isle, the island where the first European colony was established (Fort Sainte Anne on Ile La Motte).

Accommodations

■ Camping

There are various places actually on Mount Mansfield where you can spend the night, either camping, in a lean-to or in a shelter.

Underhill State Camping Area (Underhill State Park, Underhill Center, Vermont, 05490, ☎ 802-899-3022): Surrounding the parking area there are six lean-tos, each big enough to accommodate six people, and one of them has a wheelchair ramp. There are also ten campsites.

Services: running water (cold only), lodge and wood. The park ranger has an interesting way of distributing the wood, the longer and stronger your arms the more wood you'll get since it is $3 per armful.

Smuggler's Notch State Camping Area (☎ 802-253-4014): Right next to the parking area of the same name there are 38 campsites and 14 lean-tos which can accommodate six people each.

Services: toilets, coin-operated showers, public phone, lodge and wood.

Twin Brooks Tenting Area: This campsite is located on the Long Trail, on the west side of Mount Dewey, between Nebraska Notch and Butler Lodge. It is organized specifically for groups, but single hikers are welcome. There are tent platforms, toilets and a lodge, and it is all free!

Gold Brook Campground: (on Route 16 near Stowe, ☎ 802-253-7683): Open year round.

■ Lodges

Taylor Lodge: Constructed in 1978, in memory of James P. Taylor, one of the founders of the Green Mountain Club, Taylor Lodge can fit about 20 people per night. If it is full, there is always room on the balcony. There is water on the Lake Mansfield trail (at 400 m). If the ranger comes by the fee is $4 per night. The lodge is accessible from Stevensville via the Nebraska Notch Trail and the Long Trail. It is an easy, two-hour hike.

Butler Lodge: This log-cabin style lodge was built in 1933. It was later named in memory of Mabel Taylor Butler who was a member of the Burlington chapter of the Green Mountain Club and a lover of the area. There is a spectacular view of the summits of the Green Mountains to the south and of the Lake Champlain Valley and the Adirondacks to the west. The lodge can accommodate 15 people and is supervised during the summer. It is accessible via the Butler Trail from Stevensville in about two hours.

Taft Lodge: Constructed in 1920, this is the oldest lodge on the Long Trail. Its 32-person capacity also makes it the largest. There is water located right next to the lodge, follow the signs, and a view of the White Mountains to the east. The lodge is located just under the "chin" of Mount Mansfield. Off Route 108 from Stowe, take the Long Trail heading west. The trail up to the lodge is only slightly uphill and takes about two hours to complete. The lodge is supervised in the summer.

■ **Hotels, Motels, Inns ...**

Smuggler's Notch

Smuggler's Notch Resort (☎ 802-644-8851): Like a self-contained village, complete with pools, sauna, hot-tubs, tennis, daycare, etc.

Stowe

Green Mountain Inn (☎ 1-800-445-6629 or 802-253-7301): Situated in the centre of town, this hotel is a historic site and houses a terrific restaurant called The Whip.

The Brass Lantern Inn (717 Maple St., 05672, ☎ 1-800-729-2980 or 802-253-2229): Bed & Breakfast, comfortable atmosphere (9 rooms), non-smoking.

Short Hikes

■ **Mount Mansfield**

Haselton Trail

Level of difficulty:	
Total distance:	*6.8 km*
Time:	*4 h*
Change in altitude:	*780 m*
Starting point:	*parking lot of the Mount Mansfield Ski Touring Center, on Route 108.*

The Haselton Trail, one of the oldest trails on Mount Mansfield, goes up the eastern slope to the Nose summit, or to Summit Station.

It has a gradual incline, crosses a stream, downhill ski trails, and arrives finally at the Toll road, which leads cars up to the summit (there is, as the name suggests, a toll).

If you follow the road it is only another 800 m to the Summit Station and the Long Trail. Following the "Triangle Trail", which leads directly to the Nose, is another option. Return by the same trail.

Sunset Ridge

Level of difficulty:	
Total distance:	*10 km*
Time:	*4 h 30 min*
Change in altitude:	*622 m*
Starting point:	*Underhill State Camping Area.*

This magnificent trail leads to the summit of Mount Mansfield, also known as The Chin. Most of the trail is located above the timberline and therefore provides a look at a good variety of the vegetation and shows how it changes with altitude.

The beginning of the trail is quite steep. As the vegetation becomes less dense the trail becomes less steep. While still walking through forest you will pass a small sign indicating the way to Cantilever Rock. If you have time (it only takes about 15 minutes) follow the trail and check out this interesting rock formation: basically a horizontal obelisk projecting from a rock wall about 18 m from the ground.

On the way up there are various picnic spots, the nicest is on a smooth inclined rock beside the trail just below the timberline. Since most of the trail is above the timberline, it is important to bring along a windbreaker and warm clothes.

Butler Lodge

Level of difficulty:	🏔🏔
Total distance:	*7.2 km*
Time:	*5 h 30 min*
Change in altitude:	*774 m*
Starting point:	*Stevensville.*

The trail is uneventful up to Butler Lodge, climbing steadily through forest the whole way. Despite the lack of excitement it is still a pleasant trail, not too steep and well maintained.

For some, the hike will end at Butler Lodge and its lookout over the village of Underhill Center. For others this will be a rest stop on their way up to The Forehead. The second part of the trail is much more uneven and steep. There are even a few ladders at the steeper sections.

The more dangerous and thrilling sections of the trail are guaranteed to send chills up your spine, but do not get over-excited, as particular caution is necessary in rainy weather when these rocks become very slippery. The area of The Forehead is within the alpine vegetation zone. If you still have time and energy once you get there continue up to the Summit Station for a look at the other slope. Return by the same trail or follow Maple Ridge and Frost Trail down.

Laura Cowles

Level of difficulty:	🏔🏔🏔
Total distance:	*8.6 km*
Time:	*5 h*
Change in altitude:	*622 m*
Starting point:	*Underhill State Camping Area.*

Contrary to Sunset Ridge which follows a ridge, the Laura Cowles Trail goes straight up the west side of Mount Mansfield. It is more protected from the wind, but as the incline is much steeper, the trail is quite difficult. It crosses two streams which may present a problem depending on water levels. In hot weather though you will probably welcome the opportunity for a nice dip.

This trail is usually used when bad weather makes Sunset Ridge too risky, or as a quick way down in any weather. All the trails converge in the upper section of Laura Cowles; watch for the signs. Return by the same trail, Sunset Ridge or Halfway House Trail.

Halfway House

Level of difficulty:	
Total distance:	*8 km*
Time:	*4 h*
Change in altitude:	*470 m*
Starting point:	*Underhill State Camping Area.*

This trail is ideal for the hiker who wants to get up to the ridge on a rough trail, but does not want to expend too much energy. The trail consists of a series of switchbacks, so it is not too steep and ideal for the whole family. There is no water on the way so fill up before starting out. Return by the same trail, Sunset Ridge or Laura Cowles.

Subway

Level of difficulty:	
Total distance:	*0.5 km*
Time:	*15 min*
Change in altitude:	*100 m*
Starting point:	*the ridge (Tundra Trail).*

A great way to really explore the western slope, this is a short fifteen minute trail. There are a few precarious stretches, and ladders are provided at the real tough spots. Do not venture here during a storm, especially if there is lightning.

Long Trail

Level of difficulty:	⌃⌃
Total distance:	*7.4 km*
Time:	*5 h 15 min*
Change in altitude:	*850 m*
Starting point:	*Route 108.*

From the road the trail climbs straight up to Taft Lodge. It is a pleasant walk up and allows a good look at the changing vegetation. The trail presents no particular difficulties, and there is water available along the way.

Once at the shelter, you may want to stop and rest, have a bite to eat and take in the magnificent view. From the shelter there are two possible routes up to The Chin: the Long Trail to the right of the Lodge, or the Profanity Trail to the left. The Long Trail climbs steadily up to the pass between the summit and the Adam's Apple. It then gets steeper and actually quite challenging in spots. If you opt for the Profanity Trail, you will soon discover the reason for its name: it is very steep! Rhythm and pacing are key here to avoiding complete exhaustion before reaching the summit.

Note: This trail is an excellent alternative if the weather becomes too rough for Sunset Ridge. A loop-trail is also possible by hiking up the Long Trail and down Profanity Trail.

Tundra Trail

Level of difficulty:	⌃
Total distance:	*4.2 km*
Time:	*1 h 15 min*
Change in altitude:	*165 m*
Starting point:	*from one of the trails along the ridge or the Stowe chairlift*

This trail is unique in Vermont. You will feel as though you are 2,250 km to the north of your actual location, somewhere around Hudson's Bay, because the trail is situated entirely in an arctic-alpine vegetation zone, unchanged since the retreat of the last glaciers which once covered all of North America.

The junction with Halfway House Trail is above the timberline. Here the trees grow almost horizontally and twisted. They hug the ground to avoid exposure to the elements. Trees that grow vertically inevitably lose their top branches in the wind.

In the 19th century, Halfway House Trail was a horse trail used to transport people from the Halfway House Hotel, in Underhill, to the Summit House. Though it is no longer frequented by horses, it remains one of the most popular trails on the mountain. During the summer months you will notice small white flowers growing all over the ridge. These are sand lilies, a wild flower of the arctic-alpine regions.

Near the summit is a pile of stones known as "Frenchman's Pile". Legend has it that many years ago a man was struck and killed by lightning on this spot; it serves today as a warning to hikers on this ridge. If you do find yourself in the middle of a lightning storm, get out of the open, and take cover in the forest immediately.

Summit Station

The parking lot at the end of the road is the site of the original Mount Mansfield Summit Station, which until 1958 was one of the most popular summit houses in New England. Visitors were brought up in sleighs to spend the night, and contemplate the sunrise. Ralph Waldo Emerson, in 1862, describes an early morning ritual where a man passed through Summit Station ringing a huge bell and crying, "sunrise". And so with everyone up, the hike up to The Nose for a sunrise breakfast could begin!

Radio Antenna

After a tour of the station you come upon Alpine Meadow. The slopes on each side of the trail are covered with Labrador Tea. It is easily identifiable by its long shiny leaves with curled edges and brown undersides. The whole plant is topped off by a tiny bouquet of white flowers.

The rocks beyond the meadow are white, which indicates that the erosion is recent. Disintegration has not yet changed their colour to grey, and green lichen has not had time to grow. The branches on the trees are stunted and grow from west to east, the direction of the prevailing wind. Even though some of the trees are between 80 and 120 years old, they rarely grow larger than 10 cm in diameter.

The Peat Bog

The area to the right is an excellent example of an alpine bog. The peat on Mount Mansfield dates from about 3000 years ago and is extremely delicate. Living within the peat bog are a multitude of arctic plants, such as mountain laurel and cotton grass.

The earth in this area remains relatively humid even in the dry season. Like most of the summits of New England, Mount Mansfield receives more precipitation than in the valleys. When the summit is enshrouded in fog, the evergreen trees trap the small drops of water that make the fog and are therefore able to retain the required level of humidity necessary for their survival.

The Erratic

The huge boulders at the summit are called erratic rock; they were carried here from somewhere else by glaciers. The grooves along the rocks shows where they were literally dragged along. The rock of Mount Mansfield is composed mainly of metamorphic rock, formed by the extended compression and heating of sedimentary rock.

Look out to the west of Lake Champlain and the Adirondacks, and imagine the landscape 400 million years ago. The whole Champlain Valley was a vast inner sea. Before the great ice ages the mountains of Vermont were as much as 500 m higher than they are now. Constant erosion by wind, rain and ice have changed these mountains into what we see today. Two, maybe even three, glaciations have moulded Vermont's Green Mountains. The most recent took place about 10,000 years ago, and is primarily responsible for the region's present geography.

Hell Brook Trail

Level of difficulty:	⛰ ⛰ ⛰
Total distance:	*8-km loop*
Time:	*5 h 30 min*

Change of altitude: *792 m*
Starting point: *Route 108 (near Big Spring), 14 km south of highway 15, at Jeffersonville*

The Hell Brook Trail climbs the northeast side of Mount Mansfield. It is considered one of the more difficult trails in the Green Mountains because it requires sustained effort and follows the rocky crest of the mountainside almost continuously.

The starting point of the trail is across Route 108 from the parking area at Big Spring. Right at the beginning of the hike, the trail on the east side climbs sharply along the ridge, leading to several rocky ledges as well as to some stunning views.

After rising more than 500 metres, the trail leads to a crossing (1.4 km). The trail on the left is the Hell Brook Cutoff, a rather easy path leading to the Taft Lodge. A little further along (2.1 km) is another crossing. Take the Adam's Apple Trail on the left to enjoy a magnificent view of the Chin of Mount Mansfield as well as the eastern side of the mountain. This trail runs only 300 metres before reaching the Long Trail. Hikers who don't take the Adam's Apple Trail will go the same 300-metre distance before reaching the Long Trail (2.4 km).

The Long Trail leads to the Chin summit of Mount Mansfield (at an altitude of 1,340 metres) with just a few minutes' effort (2.9 km). Going down by the Hell Brook Trail is not advised because of its steep incline and slippery conditions after rain. It is much preferable to take the Long Trail down to Taft Lodge (3.8 km) and Route 108 (6.6 km). At the highway, go left to return to the starting point at Big Spring (8 km).

Maple Ridge Trail

Level of difficulty:
Total distance: *8.3-km loop*
Time: *5 hours*
Change of altitude: *777 m*
Starting point: *at the end of Stevensville Road. From Underhill Center, take Pleasant Valley Road and then go right on Stevensville Road.*

This loop leads up to the southwest ridge of Mount Mansfield to the southern peak called the Forehead, then heads back down by the Long

Trail toward the south. There are several excellent viewpoints along this loop, which crosses vast expanses of rock.

From the parking area, follow the small road and take the Frost Trail 300 metres along on the left. The Frost Trail rises continuously to reach the Maple Ridge Trail (2.2 km). (The Maple Ridge Trail actually begins 600 metres further down, at the end of CCC Road, if you are coming from Underhill State Camping.)

A little further, the trail comes to a crossing with the Rock Garden Trail and then climbs to a ledge, reaching another intersection (3.7 km), where the Maple Ridge Trail ends. From there it becomes the Wampahoofus Trail and climbs directly to the southern peak of Mount Mansfield (4 km), named the Forehead (1,195 m).

From the Forehead, take the Long Trail south toward Butler Lodge. The trail descends about 300 metres there and reaches a crossing (5.3 km), where you should take the Butler Lodge Trail on the right. This trail leads to the lodge of the same name, built in 1933, and continues directly down to the starting point (8.3 km).

Variation: from the Forehead, take the Long Trail north to reach the Nose summit, where you will find the Mount Mansfield Visitor Center. This round trip adds 2.6 km to the total length of this trip.

■ **Spruce Peak**

Elephant's Head

Level of difficulty:	⌂⌂⌂
Total distance:	*7.8 km*
Time:	*3 hours*
Change of altitude:	*457 m*
Starting point:	*from the parking area at the Smuggler's Notch picnic area, along Route 108, 15.2 km south of Route 15, at Jeffersonville.*

The Elephant's Head Trail leads to a marvellous viewpoint high above the narrow Smuggler's Notch passage. Make sure the little spur trail is open: it is usually closed during the spring and summer because of the falcons nesting there (check with the Green Mountain Club, ☎ 802-244-7037).

The Elephant's Head Trail leads up to the northwest point of Spruce Peak (1,000 m), with its superb viewpoint. This trail does not reach the top of Spruce Peak (although it is possible to extend the hike and reach the top of the slopes at this ski resort.

From the starting point at the picnic area, the trails crosses Notch Creek and then climbs the south side of Spruce Peak rather sharply. It crosses a ravine where a landslide once took place, and offers fine views. Further along, the trail follows the partly wooded southern ridge and leads to a crossing (3.7 km). Head left along the spur trail that goes down to the Elephant's Head ledge, above the 300-metre cliff that towers over Smuggler's Notch (3.9 km). The return is via the same trail.

■ **Mount Hunger**

Level of difficulty:	🏔🏔
Total distance:	*6.2 km*
Time:	*3 h 30 min*
Change of altitude:	*706 m*
Starting point:	*Take Guptil Road from Waterbury Center along Route 100, turning right at Maple Street and continuing to Loomis Hill, where you turn right again and then go left at the fork. There is parking on the right side of the road. A sign marks the Waterbury Trail. The parking area is 6.2 km from Route 100.*

Mount Hunger is located southeast of Mount Mansfield and forms part of the Worcester Range. With its northern and southern summits, it offers exceptional views of the area, especially of Mount Mansfield, Camel's Hump and the White Mountains. With its fairly short but rather steep trail, its superb panoramas and its blueberries in season, Mount Hunger has become a local classic.

The Waterbury Trail starts at the end of the parking area. Relatively flat at first, it cuts through forest, becoming steeper and crossing a creek (1.4 km). As it keeps climbing, the trail crosses a second creek (1.9 km) and a third (2.4 km). Just a little further, a crossing appears (2.7 km). The trail on the right leads to White Rock Mountain (974 m).

Continuing straight, the Waterbury Trail climbs to the rocky southern summit of Mount Hunger (3.1 km). Identify this trail clearly to avoid any confusion when returning. This 1,079-metre summit offers an incredible view of the valley, the Waterbury reservoir, Camel's Hump to the southwest, Mount Mansfield to the northwest, the Worcester Range and even the White Mountains of New Hampshire to the east. Return by the same trail. (Take note of the different trails that meet at the summit to avoid going the wrong way when returning.)

■ Stowe Pinnacle Mountain

Level of difficulty:	
Total distance:	*4.6 km*
Time:	*2 h 30 min*
Change of altitude:	*463 m*
Starting point:	*Heading south from the village of Stowe along Route 100, take Gold Brook Road. Go left at the first fork and continue to the second intersection, with Upper Hollow Road, where you turn right. Continue to the small parking area on the left, marked by a sign. The parking area is 3.7 km from Route 100.*

Stowe Pinnacle Mountain is one of those little mountains offering great views. Located just north of Mount Hunger, it is also part of the Worcester Range.

The trail begins next to the parking area and crosses big fields. Flat at first, it becomes steeper later on and snakes through the forest. It is heavily used and easy to follow. Further along, it leads to a small peak below the summit (1.4 km). A small and very short spur trail leads on the left to a pretty lookout.

The trail goes around the summit toward the north and becomes almost flat. Climbing somewhat after this, the trail then comes to an intersection (1.9 km). The Skyline Trail arrives here to the left. Go right, and continue climbing to reach the rocky summit of Stowe Pinnacle Mountain (2.3 km).

From the summit (808 m), the view extends in all directions. Mount Mansfield stands in all its glory to the west, while Camel's Hump, to the southwest, is easy to spot. Return by the same trail.

 Long Hikes

Even though Mount Mansfield does not spread out to cover a huge area, some long hikes with overnights are still possible. Most of these are along the Long Trail, since it is the only trail long enough to spend two days on!

■ **Mount Mansfield**

Long Trail

Level of difficulty:	
Total distance:	*17.8 km*
Time:	*2 days*
Change in altitude:	*622 m*
Starting point:	*Taylor Lodge.*

There are two options for this hike. You could either depart the evening before Day One, leaving the car in Stevensville and hiking two hours along Nebraska Notch to Taylor Lodge to spend the night. Or if you decide to depart on Day One, be sure to get an early start after leaving your car in Stevensville. From Taylor Lodge head towards Butler Lodge to join up with the Long Trail.

Day One: In order to take full advantage of the day, an early start is key. The trail is not difficult to follow between Taylor Lodge and Taft Lodge, where you will spend the night.

From Taylor Lodge either backtrack to the intersection of the Long Trail and Nebraska Notch and then continue to the north along the Long Trail, or follow the Clara Bow Trail which leads eventually to the Long Trail. This little trail winds through the rocks and is worth the detour.

Continue on the Long Trail all the way to Butler Lodge, where you might stop for a break or a bite to eat. Continue up to the Summit Station, the

Tundra Trail and the summit (The Chin). Then, it is downhill to the Taft Lodge for the night.

Day Two: this will be an easy day. There are several options, either hike directly down to Route 108, hike back up to the summit and then return to the Underhill State Camping Area via Sunset Ridge, or return to Stevensville by the CCC Road and the Frost Trail. This last option will lengthen the hike.

Loop from Underhill State Camping Area

Level of difficulty:	
Total distance:	*9.9 km*
Time:	*2 days*
Change in altitude:	*622 m*
Starting point:	*Underhill State Camping Area.*

When arriving in the evening, spend the night at the Underhill State Camping Area.

Day One: The first day is short, leaving plenty of time to admire the landscape and the beautiful alpine flora. The lodge is reached early, with plenty of time to prepare a good supper.

Along Sunset Ridge is the intersection of the Long Trail and the Profanity Trail. There are two options at this point, either hike straight up to The Chin, or head back down via Profanity to Taft Lodge for the night. At the summit either backtrack over the Profanity Trail to Taft Lodge or follow the Long Trail to the north and then down to Taft Lodge.

Day Two: The distance to cover on day two is longer, but it is over mostly flat terrain on the main ridge. Along the Tundra Trail watch out for the fragile vegetation.

From Taft Lodge hike up to the summit via the Long Trail or the Profanity Trail, then head south along the Long Trail to The Forehead. Between the summit and the Summit Station you are following the Tundra Trail, refer to the description of this trail earlier in the guide for information on the area. From The Forehead follow the Maple Ridge Trail and the CCC Road back to the Underhill State Camping Area.

Camel's Hump

Camel's Hump may be the most delightful mountain in all of Vermont. Its unusual shape, its numerous trails and, above all, the exceptional view from its bald summit make it a very special spot for nature lovers.

Camel's Hump is not the highest mountain in Vermont nor the second highest, but reaching an altitude of 1,245 metres it shares third place with Mount Ellen, about 30 km south.

The first people to name this mountain may have been Waubanaukee Indians, who gave it the name Tah-wak-be-dee-ee-wadso, meaning "saddle mountain". The French explorer Samuel de Champlain gave this mountain the name *le lion couchant*, meaning "sleeping lion". The current name comes from Camel's Rump, which appeared on a historical map in 1798. In 1830, the name was changed to Camel's Hump.

With its bare top, this mountain stands out from a distance, notably from Huntington Center. The hump sticking out from the forest is clearly visible, and it is easy to imagine the captivating views that await at the top.

This fabulous mountain is part of the Camel's Hump State Park and is protected against excessive development. It is the only peak more than 4,000 feet high not to have suffered transformations such as a ski resort or a road to the top. The history of Camel's Hump State Park began in 1911, when Col. Joseph Battell offered the State of Vermont 1,000 acres of forest, including the Camel's Hump mountain. Nowadays the park has grown to more than 20,000 acres. This zone was declared a State Natural Area by Vermont in 1965 and a National Natural Landmark by the U.S. federal government three years later.

Camel's Hump is topped by fragile alpine-arctic vegetation. Mounts Mansfield and Abraham, along with Camel's Hump, are the only mountains in Vermont with this type of vegetation. It is thus fully appropriate to ask hikers to stay on the trails and not to pick any plants or flowers. Camping is forbidden, of course, and dogs must be kept leashed. Caretakers are often posted at the summit, or close by to acquaint hikers with this vegetation. It should be noted that more than 20,000 hikers climb to the top of Camel's Hump each year.

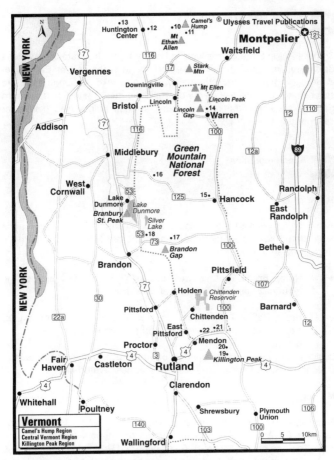

Camel's Hump Region	Central Vermont Region	Killington Peak Region
10. Camel's Hump View Trail 11. Estern Loop 12. Western Loop 13. Audubon Nature Center 14. Mount Abraham 15. Texas Falls 16. Robert Frost Trail	17. Mount Horrid 18. Falls of Lana	19. Killington Peak 20. Pico Peak 21. Deer Leap Mountain 22. Blue Ridge Mountain

Finding Your Way Around

Camel's Hump State Park is located just south of Interstate 89 between Burlington and Montpelier. Take Exit 11 at Richmond or Exit 10 at Waterbury, depending on the trail you plan to take. Although there are several parking areas and plenty of trails, the main eastern and western parking areas are the recommended starting points (see below for descriptions of the trails).

 Accommodations

■ **Camping**

When the lodges are full, camping is allowed nearby. Two campgrounds with platforms and group accommodations are located near Camel's Hump. These are:

- **Hump Brook Tenting Area**: accessible by the east side of the mountain via the Forestry and Dean trails.

- **Honey Hollow Tenting Area**: located northwest of the mountain, along the Long Trail, west of Gorham Lodge.

Besides from these campgrounds along the trails, the nearest one is at Little River State Park (☎ 802-244-7103), near Waterbury.

■ **Lodges**

Four lodges are available to hikers. Two of them, Birch Glen Camp and Cowle's Cove Shelter, are located south of the park, along the Long Trail. The two others, Montclair Glen Lodge and Gorham Lodge, are also located along the Long Trail, the former being south of Camel's Hump and the latter north of the mountain. There is a charge for use of the lodges, and reservations are not accepted. Visitors may stay a maximum of two nights in each lodge.

Short Hikes

■ **Camel's Hump**

Camel's Hump View Trail

Level of difficulty:	
Total distance:	*1.3 km loop*
Time:	*45 min*
Change in altitude:	*20 m*
Starting point:	*See "The Eastern Loop" (below). Just before the parking lot for the Eastern Loop, turn left and cross the little wooden bridge.*

This short trail offers some lovely views of the summit of Camel's Hump. The path is wide and very well maintained, making it suitable even for wheelchairs. It makes a small loop, running alongside the Sinnott River part of the way. Benches have been placed in shady spots and in open areas affording a view of the bare mountaintop.

The Eastern Loop

Level of difficulty:	
Total distance:	*12-km loop*
Time:	*6 h*
Change in altitude:	*806 m*
Starting point:	*Interstate 89, Exit 10 (Waterbury). Take Route 2 into the village of Waterbury and turn right on Route 100, then immediately right again on River Road. Stay to the right and continue along this road, which runs alongside the river for about 7 km. Take a left on Camel's Hump Road and continue uphill for nearly 6 km, to the parking lot for the Forestry Trail.*

This loop, composed of the Forestry, Dean and Long Trails, covers the east side of Camel's Hump. Given the route's popularity with North American hikers, solitude is pretty much out of the question. Nevertheless, following this hike through to the end is well worth the effort.

The parking lot is located at a place called Couching Lion Farm, which was given to the state by W.S. Monroe. Several types of trees from other regions can be found here. At the far end of the parking lot, on the left, there is a plaque commemorating the dramatic events of 1942, when an airplane crashed near the top of the mountain.

Start off on the Forestry Trail, which leads from the parking lot through the forest. This part of the hike is easy, and you'll soon find yourself at an intersection (2.1 km). Head left on the Dean Trail, which leads across Hump Brook (2.4 km), near the Hump Brook Tenting Area, equipped with platforms where you can set up your tent for the night. Farther along, you'll come across an excellent demonstration of beaver know-how (3.2 km) and enjoy a view of the summit of Camel's Hump.

After the beaver pond, the trail leads uphill to an intersection at an opening known as the Wind Gap (3.7 km). At this point the Dean Trail ends, and hikers can pick up the Long Trail or the Allis Trail. Those wishing to go to the Montclair Glen Lodge, a little over 300 m away, should head left on the Long Trail South. Otherwise, head right on the Long Trail to reach the top of Camel's Hump.

On its way to the summit, the Long Trail passes along rock faces, offering lovely views of the pond and the valley. Farther along, it gets steeper and intersects with the Alpine Trail (6.1 km). The latter, coming in from the right, offers a safer way to skirt round the summit in bad weather. After the intersection, the trail leads straight to the bare summit of Camel's Hump (6.4 km). Make sure to stay on the trail, as the alpine-arctic vegetation in this area is extremely fragile.

The view from the rocky summit of Camel's Hump (1,245 m) is one of the most beautiful in all of Vermont. To the south, Pico Peak and Mounts Ethan Allen, General Stark, Lincoln and Killington stand out against the horizon. To the north, you'll see Mount Mansfield (1,340 m), the highest peak in Vermont; the Worcester Range, Belvidere Mountain and Mount Owl's Head, in Quebec. To the east, you can make out the White Mountains (New Hampshire), and to the west, the Adirondacks (New York).

From the summit, continue north on the Long Trail. On the way back down, you'll come to an intersection (6.9 km). Head right on the Forestry Trail, which leads down to the parking lot. You'll reach two intersections on the way; the second (9.8 km) is the same one you passed at the beginning of the hike (Dean Trail). At this point, you are only 2.2 km from where you started.

The Western Loop

Level of difficulty:	🔼🔼🔼
Total distance:	*9-km loop*
Time:	*5 h*
Change in altitude:	*665 m*
Starting point:	*Interstate 89, Exit 11. Take Route 2 to Richmond. At the light, turn right on Bridge Street and head to Huntington and then Huntington Center. In Huntington Center, take Camel's Hump Road to the end (5.6 km), to the main parking lot (after the first, smaller parking lot).*

The Western Loop is made up of the Forest City, Long and Burrows Trails. Like the Eastern Loop, it's a classic in this region.

From the parking lot, start off the loop on the Burrows Trail. Almost immediately after, however, you must turn right on the Burrows-Forest City Connector, which leads to the Forest City Trail. This short cut enables you to skip the beginning of the Forest City Trail, which starts lower, at the first parking lot.

When you get to the Forest City Trail, turn left. The path climbs gently up intersection with the Long Trail (2.1 km) at a point known as the Wind Gap. The nearby Montclair Glen Lodge, built in 1948, can accommodate up to 10 hikers.

At the intersection, head left on the Long Trail, toward the summit of Camel's Hump, whose rock faces offer a lovely view of the pond and the valley. Farther along, the trail gets steeper and intersects with the Alpine Trail, which comes in from the right. After the intersection, the Long Trail leads straight to the bare summit of Camel's Hump (5.1 km). Make sure to stay on the path, as the alpine-arctic vegetation in this area is extremely fragile.

The view from the rocky summit of Camel's Hump (1,245 m) is one of the most beautiful in all of Vermont. To the south, Pico Peak and Mounts Ethan Allen, General Stark, Lincoln and Killington stand out against the horizon. To the north, you'll see Mount Mansfield (1,340 m), the highest peak in Vermont; the Worcester Range, Belvidere Mountain and Mount Owl's Head, in Quebec. To the east, you can make out the White Mountains (New Hampshire), and to the west, the Adirondacks (New York).

From the summit, continue north on the Long Trail. At the intersection (5.6 km), head left on the Burrows Trail, which leads down the western ridge of Camel's Hump to the parking lot (9 km).

■ Audubon Nature Center

Level of difficulty:	
Total distance:	*several small loops totalling 8 km*
Time:	*between 15 and 60 minutes for each loop*
Change of altitude:	*maximum of 60 metres*
Starting point:	*The centre, whose full name is Green Mountain Audubon Nature Center, is located at 255 Sherman Hollow Road in Huntington, ☎ (802) 434-3068. Take Exit 11 from Interstate 89 and then Route 2 to Richmond. At the traffic light, go right on Bridge Street toward Huntington. After about 8 km, go right on Sherman Hollow Road, where there is a sign marking the centre, located nearby on the left.*

The centre belongs to the National Audubon Society, an organization founded in 1905 and dedicated to the protection of birdlife. It takes its name from John J. Audubon (1785-1851), and American naturalist and painter. The Vermont chapter of the Audubon Society, created in 1962, aims to protect flora and fauna while also raising public awareness through environmental education programs. It has more than 1,000 members and more than 400 volunteers. The centre receives over 30,000 visitors each year, as well as various groups from schools and summer camps.

The centre's reception area occupies a superb farmhouse donated by Christine L. Hires in 1964 to serve the Audubon Society. Mrs. Hires also donated other buildings as well as 60 hectares (150 acres) of land. Today the centre has been expanded and has 93 hectares (230 acres) of land on both sides of the highway, extending to the Huntington River.

Before heading along the trails, hikers will want to visit the reception area to obtain the various leaflets and a free map of the trails. It also has a small gift shop and interactive displays of fauna and flora. When the reception area is closed, leaflets are available in the barn near the parking area.

Among the ten trails, we can suggest the Hires Trails, named, of course, for the donor of this spot. This hike of about 35 minutes, goes up the hill behind the house and offers superb views of Camel's Hump, which reaches an altitude of 1,245 metres. It is also possible to see Mount Mansfield (1,340 m) on the left.

The Sensory Trail (30 minutes), with the starting point next to the house, provides an unforgettable experience. All along this trail, a rope serves as a handrail and shows the way. For an interesting walk, blindfold yourself and follow the trail as a blind person would, using the senses of touch, sound and smell!

On the other side of Sherman Hollow Road are trails leading to beaver ponds, a white pine forest and a sugar shack, as well as one along the beautiful Huntington River.

Central Vermont

 Short Hikes

■ Mount Abraham

Level of difficulty:	🏔️🏔️
Total distance:	*8.4 km*
Time:	*4 hours*
Change of altitude:	*482 m*
Starting point:	*from Lincoln Gap, located halfway (7.5 km) between the villages of Warren (Route 100) and Lincoln, reached by Lincoln Gap Road (closed in the winter).*

The trail referred to here forms part of the Long Trail North. It climbs onto a little butte and then descends through a small pass. The climb to the ridge of Mount Abraham really begins at this point (0.6 km) and offers some steeper sections. Climbing onto a rocky ledge, the trail emerges at a small west-facing lookout and then returns to the forest.

Further along, the trail passes between two big boulders nicknamed Carpenters (1.9 km) and leads to a lookout facing Mount Abraham. The trail becomes flatter, crosses a creek and arrives at a crossing (2.7 km). The Battel Trail from the west also runs here along the ridge. The Long Trail turns right and goes up to the Battell Shelter. This lodge, built in 1967, can accommodate eight hikers for the night. A caretaker is often on the site.

From the lodge, the trail first follows a former road and then climbs more sharply onto some rocks and leads to the bare summit of Mount Abraham (4.2 km). The extraordinary view from there (1,221 m) is considered one of the most spectacular along the Long Trail. The White Mountains to the east, Killington Peak to the south, the Adirondacks to the west, Belvidere Mountain to the north and several other peaks can all be contemplated.

Note that the summit of Mount Abraham has a very fragile arctic-alpine type of vegetation. Hikers are strongly urged to stay on the trail to avoid damaging this growth, which is very rare in Vermont. Mount Abraham is one of only three mountains in Vermont with this type of vegetation, Mount Mansfield and Camel's Hump being the others. Return by the same trail.

■ Texas Falls

Level of difficulty:
Total distance: *1.9-km loop*
Time: *1 hour*
Change of altitude: *50 m*
Starting point: *From the village of Hancock (along Route 100), go 5 km south along Route 125, turning right along the side road at the sign marked Texas Falls Recreation Area. Go 800 metres until the little parking area on the left. (Note that there is also a bigger parking area with picnic tables 400 metres further along.)*

Texas Falls are a group of delightful little waterfalls in a peaceful setting where nature seems to take things easy. With an immense picnic area near the Hancock River (some of the tables are sheltered from the rain by a big roof), and with its interesting little trail, Texas Falls make for a first-rate rest stop.

The starting point is just across the road. The sound of the falls can be heard even at the parking area. Hikers can obtain headsets explaining the history and environment of the falls (no leaflets were available during our visit in May 1996).

After observing the falls across the little bridge, take the trail on the left along the Hancock River. This river flows into the White River, which in turn flows into the Connecticut River at the state line between Vermont and New Hampshire. After 0.5 km, the trail runs near the main parking area, which has a picnic area. Then it swings right and climbs into the forest, turning south and heading back down toward the falls (1.6 km). Near the falls, a small spur trail leads to a pretty viewpoint over the falls and the gorge. Back at the main trail, turn left to reach the little bridge and return to the starting point (1.9 km).

■ **Robert Frost Trail**

Level of difficulty:	
Total distance:	*1.6-km loop*
Time:	*1 hour*
Change of altitude:	*35 m*
Starting point:	*From the town of Hancock (Route 100), take Route 125 for 15,7 km to the sign on the left indicating "Robert Frost Trail". (From the town of Ripton, drive 3,4 km, the parking lot will be on the right.) There is a terrific picnic spot on the other side of the road called "Robert Frost Wayside", it is set in a magnificent pine forest.*

Robert Frost (1874-1963) was an American poet who came to live in this beautiful part of Vermont. Honoured officially by the State of Vermont, Robert Frost was also named First Citizen of the little town of Ripton.

The pretty little trail created in his honour provides an enchanting setting to explore the writings of this nature poet. Plaques along the trail present some of his poems. There are also labels identifying trees and plants.

At the starting point, a signboard provides information about the poet and about the trail. To the right, the trail leads along a little passageway in the forest above a small marsh. Note that the first part of the trail forms a loop and is accessible to wheelchairs.

Further along, turn right again and take the little wooden bridge across the Middlebury River. Beyond the bridge, go right again. The trail climbs very slightly into the forest and leads to a crossing, where you should continue straight. The trail then goes back down and leads to a superb meadow (0.8 km). A sign indicates the various mountains that are visible in the distance. Running along the river and the meadow, the trails returns to the little bridge. After crossing the bridge, turn right and continue along the trail, which soon returns to the parking area (1.6 km).

■ **Mount Horrid**

Level of difficulty:	◢◣
Total distance:	*2.4 km*
Time:	*1 hour*
Change of altitude:	*188 metres*
Starting point:	*at the parking area located atop Brandon Gap. Arriving from the east along Route 100, take Route 73 south of Rochester over a distance of 14.8 km, to the summit of Brandon Gap where the Long Trail parking area is located. If you are coming from the west, the parking area is located 13.2 km from Route 7 in Brandon.*

Mount Horrid is a 980-metre-high mountain traversed by the famous Long Trail. The suggested hike does not reach the summit but does go to the superb cliff that forms the south side of Mount Horrid. Called the Great Cliff, it sits 200 metres above the Brandon breach. Note that the site is usually closed in the spring (and sometimes right up to the beginning of August) because of falcons nesting there.

For a magnificent view of the cliff, hikers can walk or drive first to the small parking area located east of the Long Trail parking area, with very pretty views of the cliff and a small pond. It is easy to imagine the spectacle that awaits at the top of this cliff.

The trail starts on the other side of Route 73. Following the Long Trail North, you go along the western ridge of the mountain in a steady climb. After going through a section of forest, the trail becomes steeper and follows the rocky face of the mountain. In a clearing (1 km), a small spur trail leads to the top of this immense cliff (1.2 km). From the top of the cliff, at an altitude of 853 metres, there are impressive views of the highway below, the pond and its surroundings. Return by the same trail.

■ Falls of Lana

Level of difficulty:	⏏
Total distance:	*1.8-km loop*
Time:	*1 hour*
Change of altitude:	*75 m*
Starting point:	*at the parking area located along Route 53, south of Lake Dunmore. If you are coming from Route 7, past Middlebury, take Route 53, which runs along the eastern side of this beautiful lake. The parking area is on the left, 300 metres past Branbury State Park. Make sure you are in the parking area with a brown sign marked Trail; there is also another parking area located a little closer to the park.*

This loop allows for the exploration of a series of delightful little waterfalls as well as offering a superb view of the whole area and a spot for picnicking. You have to keep a close watch, though: this little loop crosses a number of other trails.

At the starting point, the trail climbs somewhat and soon reaches a side road. Go right, and follow this road until the "Green Mountain National Forest" sign. Then take the road going up on the left, leading to an immense metal tube coming down the mountain. This tube is actually a water conduit carrying water from Silver Lake to the electricity plant located along Route 53.

After passing the tube, the trail rises, passing above the Falls of Lana, located on the left. From there, it is possible to see the falls as well as Sucker Creek, which feeds them. Following the creek, the trail leads to a crossing, 800 metres from the starting point. Continue straight and take the little bridge that crosses the creek. After the bridge there is another crossing with a sign. Go left along Branbury Park Trail, leading to a picnic area. Hikers should then follow the blue markers.

At the end of the picnic area, the trail passes to the right of a big boulder and leads to another crossing. Go left, and climb along the rocks, where you will find superb views of Lake Dunmore directly below, as well as the magnificent valley and the Adirondacks in the distance.

After this lookout, continue along the rocks and go down the other side. The trail runs near the Falls of Lana, which can be observed from the rocks. It is said that the Falls of Lana got their name from General Wool, who was nicknamed General Lana, from the Spanish word for wool, during a sojourn in Mexico.

After the falls (keep following the blue markers), the trail descends on the right through the forest and then turns left, leading to a campground (1.4 km). Continue straight and turn left on Route 53. Go along the road past the tube and the electricity plant, located on the right, returning to the parking area (1.8 km).

Killington Peak Region

The Killington Peak region is located east of Rutland, Vermont's second biggest city with 18,000 inhabitants. In this charming town are a number of well-maintained old dwellings and a downtown area with several friendly restaurants and bars. Rutland has been nicknamed Marble City; its prosperity has rested on its impressive quarrying and processing operations. In the little village of Proctor, 15 km north of Rutland along Route 3, it is possible to visit the **Vermont Marble Company Exhibit** *(61 Main Street, Proctor, ☎ 802-459-2300)*, which presents the history of this industry along with several samples of rock.

Just as Rutland has the second biggest population in the state, Killington Peak (1,293 metres) is the second highest in Vermont, surpassed only by Mount Mansfield (1,340 metres). Because of the Killington and Pico Peak ski resorts, this mountain area attracts substantial crowds with the arrival of the precious white stuff. Although it is located in the southern part of the state, it is not unusual to see a plentiful accumulation of snow even into the early days of May.

 Finding Your Way Around

From Burlington, there are at least three ways to get to this area: 1) from Interstate 89, take Interstate 189 and then Route 7 south to Rutland; 2) take Interstate 89 to Waterbury and then Route 100 south to Route 4 and Sherburne Pass; 3) stay on Interstate 89 until Exit 3 (Bethel) and then take Route 107 and, finally, Route 100 south to Route 4 and Sherburne Pass.

 Accommodations

■ **Camping**

Gifford Woods State Park *(☎ 802-775-5354)*: along Route 100, just north of the junction with Route 4 (Sherburne Pass).

Killington Campground *(☎ 802-422-9787)*: along Killington Road, 4 km from Route 4.

 Short Hikes

■ **Killington Peak**

Killington Peak

Level of difficulty:	⌃⌃⌃
Total distance:	*11.6 km*
Time:	*5 h 30 min*
Change of altitude:	*755 m*

Starting point: *From Sherburne Pass (Route 4), go west almost 7 km toward Rutland, turning left onto Wheelerville Road. Follow this road for 6.4 km, until you come to a sharp curve: there is a small parking area on the left. (From Rutland, it is 10.5 km east along Route 4 to reach Wheelerville Road.)*

This peak, the second highest in Vermont, is busy all year. In the winter, skiers glide down its slopes, while in the summer hikers gather to enjoy one of the finest panoramas in the Green Mountains. The Long Trail and the Appalachian Trail, forming a single trail from the south of the state, cross Killington Peak from north to south. The trail suggested here runs along the west side of the mountain, offering a pleasant day-long hike.

The suggested trail is called the Bucklin Trail. This hike is difficult because of its length, although there are no very steep sections for the first half. From the starting point, the trail follows a small logging road and crosses a creek named Brewers Brook. It runs alongside this stream before crossing it again (1.9 km). After continuing alongside the creek, the logging road ends (3.2 km) and the trail turns right.

The trail begins to climb the steep west face of Killington Peak, leading to a crossing (5.5 km) with the Long Trail as well as to Cooper Lodge. Built in 1939, Cooper Lodge can accommodate 12 persons. Constructed of stone and wood at an altitude of 1,173 m, it is the highest shelter along the Long Trail. A caretaker is often there or near the summit to sensitize hikers to this special environment.

From this crossing, the Long Trail's Killington spur ascends directly to the rocky summit of Killington Peak (5.8 km). This mountain was named after the village of the same name at its foot (the village is now called Sherburne). From the summit (1,293 m), the view extends in all directions. You can make out Mount Mansfield to the north, Mount Ascutney to the southeast, and Lake Champlain and the Adirondacks to the west, as well as the White Mountains to the northeast. Return by the same trail.

■ Pico Peak

Level of difficulty:	◪◪
Total distance:	*9.2 km*
Time:	*4 hours*
Change of altitude:	*550 m*
Starting point:	*at the Long Trail parking area at Sherburne Pass, located 2.3 km west of the junction of Route 100 and 4. If you are coming from Rutland and Route 7, you have to go 15 km east along Route 4. Park in the biggest parking area, located on the south side of the highway facing The Inn at Long Trail.*

Pico Peak is located just north of Killington Peak. Both have popular ski resorts. The trail running along this mountain is the Long Trail, heading south.

Leaving the Sherburne Pass parking area, hikers are already at an altitude of 655 metres. The trail begins at the end of the parking area. From the Long Trail registration box, the path goes to the right and rises steadily. Further along, it meets a small spur trail leading to the ski slopes (0.9 km). Continuing on the left, the main trail rises gently and comes to a small creek named Sink Hole Brook (1.7 km).

After turning right, the trail reaches a ski slope (3.4 km). This crossing is named Pico Junction. Turn left and go about 100 metres up the slope. Since this spot is exposed, there is a view extending north and taking in the Chittenden reservoir. Going left again, the trail re-enters the forest, descending slightly and leading to Pico Camp (4 km). This lodge, built in 1959, can accommodate about a dozen hikers. A caretaker is often on site. Killington Peak is visible to the south and Mount Ascutney to the southeast of the lodge.

To climb to the top of Pico Peak, you have to take the Pico Link trail, located behind the lodge. This trail, marked in blue, rises very steeply until reaching a ski slope. The trail then turns left and leads quickly to the Pico Peak summit (4.6 km). If you walk around the summit (1,206 metres), you will find two communications towers and two lookouts with horizons sweeping northward and southward. The return is via the same trail.

Variation: from the Pico Peak summit, take the ski slope to the right, named Summit Glade. Go down this slope until the wooded crossing on the right named Pico Junction (which you will already have come upon during your ascent). Go right along the Long Trail, which descends to the parking area. This little loop at the summit reduces the total hike by 600 metres.

■ **Deer Leap Mountain**

Level of difficulty:	⌁
Total distance:	*5.6-km loop*
Time:	*2 hours*
Change of altitude:	*240 m*
Starting point:	*from the Sherburne Pass parking area (see Pico Peak above). Note that it is possible to park right next to the inn at the start of the Long Trail North.*

Take the Long Trail North, which runs along the east side of Deer Leap Mountain. (Be advised that the former trail going directly to the Deer Leap lookout is now closed.) The trail leads quickly to a cross named Maine Junction (0.8 km). This is where the Long Trail and the Appalachian Trail part ways. The Appalachian Trail leads to the right, reaching Mount Katahdin in northern Maine more than 750 km away! The Long Trail leads to the Canadian border, 269 km to the north.

Follow the Long Trail for about 60 metres, to the crossing with the Deer Leap Trail. Go left along the Deer Leap Trail, which rises directly into the forest. At the crossing (1.4 km), take the little spur trail on the left leading to the superb lookout named Little Deer Leap Lookout (1.7 km). The views of Sherburne Pass and of Pico Peak are absolutely stunning.

Back at the crossing, continue to the left along Deer Leap Trail, which soon descends a small pass and then goes up toward the wooded summit of Deer Leap Mountain (2.5 km). From there, the trail goes back down the north side of the mountain until the crossing with the Long Trail (3.5 km). Go right along the Long Trail, returning to Maine Junction (4.8 km) and from there to the parking area (5.6 km).

Variation: the round trip to the Little Deer Leap Lookout is worthwhile for its pretty scenery, and it can make for a very pleasant picnic. This hike totals 3.4 km.

■ **Blue Ridge Mountain**

Level of difficulty:	
Total distance:	*7.8 km*
Time:	*3 h 30 min*
Change of altitude:	*454 m*
Starting point:	*Go along Route 4 (6 km west of Sherburne Pass, or 9.7 km east of Route 7, at Rutland), and then take Old Turnpike Road, following it for 1.1 km until reaching a metal fence on the left.*

The trail runs first along a little road behind the fence, and is indicated by blue markers. It passes next to some campsites, crosses a small creek and followings the little logging road, leading to a little bridge (0.6 km) that runs across the creek. Further along, the trail goes left, where there is another logging road (1.4 km). The trail then becomes steeper and is lined by little cascades of water which can be quite imposing in the springtime.

The trails turns left again, becoming less difficult, and it ends up at a little clearing. Now head right, where the trail climbs to the rocky summit of Blue Ridge Mountain (3.9 km). From the main summit (1,000 m), it is preferable to continue a bit to the southwest to enjoy a better view. There, you can make out the town of Rutland and Killington Peak (1,293 m), among other sights. Return by the same trail.

The Lake Willoughby Region

Lake Willoughby is located in northeastern Vermont. About 8 km long, this lake is much appreciated by local people for its clear water, its fine beach and the big mountains that jut abruptly into the end of the lake. The cliffs that seem to strangle the southern part of the lake on either side are part of Mounts Pisgah and Hor. Fortunately for hikers, well laid-out trails run along these mountains and parts of their surroundings, offering magnificent views of the whole area.

Finding Your Way Around

From Interstate 91, take Exit 25 and go to the small town of Barton. From there, take Route 16 east to Route 5A, at the beginning of Lake Willoughby, where the beach is located. Turn right on Route 5A and continue to the village of Westmore. From there, your route will depend on your planned hike.

 Accommodations

■ **Camping**

White Caps Campground *(☎ 802-467-3345)*: along Route 5A, south of Lake Willoughby.

Will-O-Wood Campground *(☎ 802-525-3575)*: along Route 5A, south of Route 58, north of Lake Willoughby.

Belview Campground *(☎ 802-525-3242)*: along Route 16, near Barton and Crystal Lake.

 Short Hikes

■ **Mount Pisgah**

Level of difficulty:	⛰️⛰️
Total distance:	*6.2 km*
Time:	*2 h 30 min*
Change of altitude:	*442 m*
Starting point:	*the parking area along Route 5A, just south of Lake Willoughby, located on the right side of the highway. There is also a picnic area there.*

Mount Pisgah is the splendid mountain located on the southeast side of Lake Willoughby. Its immense cliff seems to jut right into the lake. In wintertime, immense ice cascades form on the side of this cliff. These

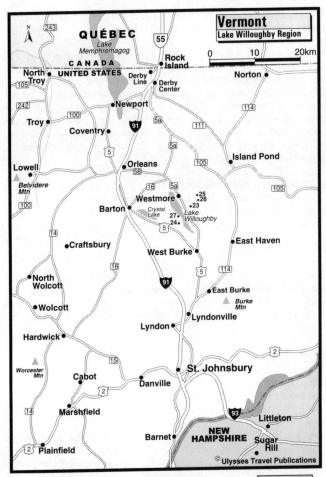

Vermont
Lake Willoughby Region

0   10   20km

QUÉBEC

Lake
Memphremagog

CANADA
UNITED STATES

North
Troy

Derby
Line

Derby
Center

Rock
Island

Norton

Newport

Troy

Coventry

Orleans

Island Pond

Lowell

Belvidere
Mtn

Westmore

•25
•26

Barton

Crystal
Lake

•23

•27
•24

Lake
Willoughby

Craftsbury

West Burke

East Haven

North
Wolcott

East Burke

Wolcott

Burke
Mtn

Lyndonville

Hardwick

Lyndon

Worcester
Mtn

Cabot

St. Johnsbury

Danville

Marshfield

Littleton

Plainfield

Barnet

NEW
HAMPSHIRE

Sugar
Hill

© Ulysses Travel Publications

Lake Willoughby Region

23. Mount Pisgah
24. Hor Mountain
25. Bald Mountain
26. Haystack Mountain
27. Mount Wheeler

ice formations, among the most beautiful in the northeastern United States, are a real treat for experienced ice climbers.

The trail along here is called the South Trail. The starting point is located on the other side of the highway. It first crosses a flooded area and then climbs steadily through the forest. It reaches the mountain ridge and then follows it continuously, intersecting with a small spur trail that leads to an exceptional lookout 1.4 km from the starting point. This lookout, nicknamed Pulpit Rock, dominates the cliff in dramatic fashion. You can observe Lake Willoughby down below as well as Mount Hor just across. Be very careful, for this little slab of rock is perched 160 metres above a sheer abyss!

Beyond the lookout, the trail continues climbing along the ridge and then plunges into the forest, reaching an uncovered spot (2.7 km) offering fine southerly views. In the distance, Burke Mountain (995 m) with its ski slopes can be seen. Just past this spot, you come to the wooded summit of Mount Pisgah (839 m). A little further along, a short spur trail leads to another lookout over the valley.

Going back down by the north side of the mountain, another spur trail, on the left, leads to a lookout called Upper Overlook (3.1 km), with views of Mount Hor, Mount Wheeler and Jay Peak, as well as Lake Willoughby and Lake Memphremagog. Return by the same trail.

■ **Mount Hor**

Level of difficulty:	
Total distance:	*5.4 km*
Time:	*2 h 30 min*
Change of altitude:	*320 m*
Starting point:	*From the parking area for the Mount Pisgah trail (see above), take CCC Road. Go right at the fork, continuing to a small parking area located on the right, 2.9 km from Route 5A.*

Mount Hor is the mountain located southwest of Lake Willoughby, directly across from Mount Pisgah. Both have steep cliffs that jut into the lake. This hike leads to three superb lookouts with views of the area, the lake and the cliffs of Mount Pisgah.

The trail is called Hawkes Trail. Part of it follows an old logging road. Although it is rather easy at the beginning, it veers left 0.6 km from the starting point and becomes progressively steeper, running through a rich forest. Just beneath the ridge near the top, it reaches a crossing (1.1 km). Take the small West Branch trail on the left, which leads to the summit. This little trail is steep but relatively short. After reaching the summit, continue along the other side of the mountain, going down a short distance to enjoy a lookout (1.6 km) that faces southwest. From there you can see numerous ponds as well as Burke Mountain (995 m).

Backtrack to the crossing (2.1 km), continuing along the trail, which changes names to East Branch. This part of the trail offers little difficulty and takes hikers to a viewpoint named East Lookout (3 km), reached by a short spur trail on the right. This spot sits atop the cliff, 350 metres above Lake Willoughby. The cliffs of Mount Pisgah are right in front.

Just after East Lookout, a trail leads down a short way north, reaching another viewpoint called North Lookout (3.2 km). The view extends across the mountain peaks of northern Vermont. The return is via the same trail, with 2.2 km remaining to reach the parking area (5.4 km).

Variation: for a shorter hike, go only as far as Summit Lookout on the West Branch, and then turn back. This 3.2-km round trip takes about 75 minutes.

■ Bald Mountain

Level of difficulty:	⛰⛰
Total distance:	*6.8 km*
Time:	*2 h 45 min*
Change of altitude:	*442 m*
Starting point:	*From Westmore, go along Route 5A, alongside the lake, and take the small, unmarked road just next to the Millbrook Store. Follow this road for 3.2 km until Long Pond. About 100 metres further, you will see a fence on the left, near which parking is possible (if not, park at Long Pond). A small white sign is marked Trail to Bald Mountain.*

Bald Mountain, reaching an altitude of 1,010 metres, is the highest peak in the area, offering superb views of the surrounding mountains and lakes. There is even an old forest ranger tower that provides a more extensive panorama.

The trail leading to the top of Bald Mountain follows former logging roads along much of its length. From the fence, the trail goes along a stretch of logging road, turning right and climbing gently. Further along, it crosses a little creek (1.6 km) and then several others (the number of creeks depends on the season). Then it crosses a bigger creek and forks to the right (2.1 km). The trail then climbs to an intersection (2.4 km), where it turns right and rises more steeply. It passes a small lookout (2.9 km) and heads left, finally reaching the summit (3.4 km). Return by the same trail. Note that at the summit there is also another trail (Lookout's Trail) going down the north side of the mountain.

■ **Haystack Mountain**

Level of difficulty:	▲
Total distance:	*3.2 km*
Time:	*1 h 30 min*
Change of altitude:	*266 m*
Starting point:	*the same access as for Bald Mountain (see above). From Long Pond, continue along the road for a little under 1 km, until reaching a small clearing on the left, where there is parking. At the end of the clearing, on one of the first trees, is a small white sign marked Haystack Trail.*

The trail presented here is named North Trail. As its name indicates, it runs along the north side of Haystack Mountain, a small rounded peak set back from the other mountains. The trail is rather easy and leads to a first lookout (1.2 km) over Bald Mountain located just to the north. At the crossing further long (1.6 km), take the little spur trail on the right, going down to a point named West Lookout. The view of Lake Willoughby and its surroundings is truly enticing. Return by the same trail.

Variation: from the West Lookout, return to the crossing and climb to the wooded mountain top (cairn), and then go a short way down the south side, coming first to the East Lookout and then to the South

Lookout, both equally spectacular. This alternative route adds only 0.6 km to the total. It is also possible to do a 5.3-km loop taking the South Trail, starting at the summit, going down to the road and returning to your car.

■ Wheeler Mountain

Level of difficulty:	
Total distance:	*3.6 km*
Time:	*1 h 45 min*
Change of altitude:	*210 m*
Starting point:	*From the village of Barton, take Route 5 south 5 km toward West Burke to the crossing with Wheeler Mountain Road. Go 3.1 km along this road (look for the Wheeler Pond Camp sign). Past two houses, a small parking area is located on the left. From this clearing, Wheeler Mountain and its rocky slabs are clearly visible. A small white sign indicates the Wheeler Trail.*

Wheeler Mountain offers what is probably the most captivating trail in the area, as well as a number of spectacular lookouts. This hike, which climbs stretches of rock on the southwest side of the mountain, will appeal in particular to children and to anyone who enjoys climbing boulders.

From the parking area, the trail follows a small road until a crossing 160 metres along. Turn right along the trail marked in red to reach the slabs of rock. (The trail marked in white is easier and bypasses this rocky area.) Climbing these slabs may seem harder than it really is. Follow the red markers: this will allow you to concentrate on the steps you are taking. If the rocks are wet, the hike will be more difficult and should be avoided, take the white trail instead.

The advantage of the steeper climb is that it allows hikers to ascend more quickly and offers fine views. The trail marked in red meets the white trail at a crossing (0.8 km) with "junction" marked on the rock. The trail rises along the ridge of the mountain, offering beautiful views, of which the most stunning (1.3 km) includes Jay Peak and Mount Mansfield.

Further along, the trail reaches the wooded summit of Wheeler Mountain (723 m) and then goes down a short distance, leading to a superb lookout called Eagle Cliff (1.8 km). The view of Lake Willoughby and of Mount Pisgah and Bald Mountain is stunning. Return by the same trail until the crossing with the junction marking. Hikers may choose to descend via the rocky slabs or to take the white trail, which is easier and only 0.3 km longer.

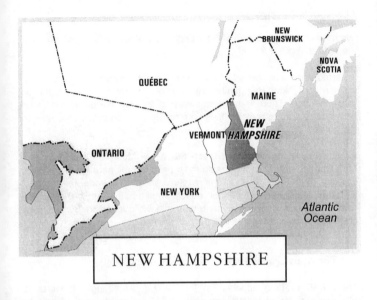

NEW HAMPSHIRE

New Hampshire, the Granite State, offers the best of both worlds, namely the mountains *and* the sea. While it only has 30 km of shoreline, the spectacular White Mountains, which cover the northern part of the state, are sure to take your breath away.

New Hampshire is the same size as Vermont but has twice the population (1,100,000). The capital, Concord (pop. 36,000) lies in the southern part of the state. The highest point in New Hampshire is imposing Mount Washington (1,917 m). The state also boasts nearly 1,300 lakes. The forests that cover over 80% of the territory have undergone radical changes over the years, with the massive felling of trees very nearly destroying most of the White Mountain region.

In 1911, however, the federal government purchased a large number of forests in order to protect them. These areas became the White Mountain National Forest, a source of great pleasure to modern-day hikers, who now roam about at will.

Politically speaking, New Hampshire has a dramatic history. This region's colonists were the first to break off all ties with England. New Hampshire thus became the first independent state in early 1776. The primary elections kicking off the race for the American presidency have been held here since 1915. Every four years, the country's attention is riveted on this little section of New England, which indicates which way the vote will go.

If Vermonters seem proud of the quality of life they strive to preserve, residents of New Hampshire are particularly proud of their political independence. There is no better way to sum up the prevailing view here than the state motto, "Live Free or Die", which you'll see all over the place.

As it takes several hours to reach the White Mountain region by car from Quebec (4 h from Montreal), most people come here for more than one day. In any case, with its many tourist attractions (mountain ridges, train trips, cable cars, museums, beaches, bike paths, etc.), this region has a great deal to offer hikers interested in discovering the rich history and natural phenomena of this part of the country.

The Appalachian Trail

The 3,640 km-long Appalachian Trail (AT) defies all logic. It starts at Mount Katahdin, in Maine, and leads 3,640 km to Mount Springer, in northern Georgia, leading through no fewer than 14 states along the way. This incredible trail was the brainchild of American philospher and writer Benton MacKaye, who came up with the idea in 1921. It took 16 years and the help of hundreds of volunteers to complete the project.

As far as the region covered by this guide is concerned, the Appalachian Trail leads through the southern part of Vermont, overlapping the Long Trail. It then heads eastward to New Hampshire, where it leads through magnificent Franconia Notch and Crawford Notch, runs along the entire southern ridge of Mount Washington and tours the lofty summits of the Presidential Range. Continuing northward, it leads into the state of Maine, threads its way between the many lakes there and finally comes to an end at famous Mount Katahdin in Baxter Park.

Appalachian Trail Conference: P.O. Box 807, Harpers Ferry, WV 25425, ☎ (304) 535-6331 (see map p 66).

Franconia Notch

This region lies west of Mount Washington, along Interstate 93, which narrows into a small road for a few kilometres. Franconia Notch is part

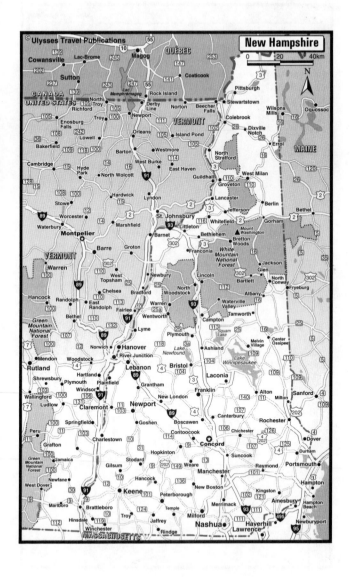

© Ulysses Travel Publications

New Hampshire

0   20   40km

N

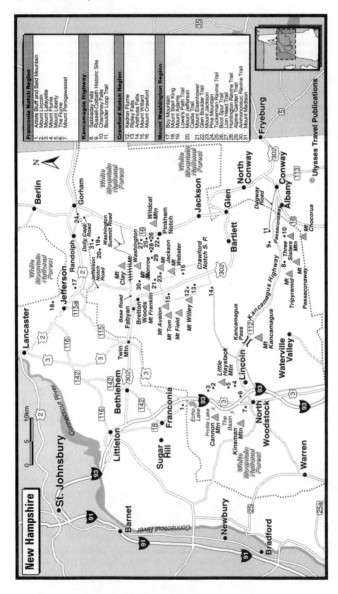

New Hampshire

Franconia Notch Region
1. Artists Bluff and Bald Mountain
2. Mount Lincoln
3. Mount Lafayette
4. Mount Flume
5. Mount Liberty
6. The Flume
7. Mount Pemigewasset

Kancamagus Highway
8. Sabbaday Falls
9. Russell-Colbath Historic Site
10. Champney Falls
11. Boulder Loop Trail

Crawford Notch Region
12. Kedron Flume
13. Ripley Falls
14. Arethusa Falls
15. Mount Willard
16. Mount Crawford

Mount Washington Region
17. Boy Mountain
18. Mount Starr King
19. Mount Adams
20. Lowe's Path Trail
20. Mount Jefferson
     Castle Trail
21. Mount Eisenhower
22. Glen Boulder Trail
23. Mount Jackson
24. Pine Mountain
25. Tuckerman Ravine Trail
26. Boot Spur Trail
27. Lion Head Trail
28. Huntington Ravine Trail
29. Alpine Garden Trail
30. Ammonoosuc Ravine Trail
31. Mount Madison

© Ulysses Travel Publications

of the state park of the same name (Franconia Notch State Park). Apparently, when cutting down trees, the first inhabitants of this part of the United States would make V-shaped notches in the trunk. When they discovered the little V-shaped mountain passes in this region, they took to calling them notches.

This narrow mountain pass stretches over 12 km from its north end, at Echo Lake, to its south end, at Flume Gorge. The Franconia Range crowds in on the valley to the east, the Kinsman to the west. The highest peak in the region is Mount Lafayette, at over 1,600 m.

The Franconia Notch region is popular with tourists and hikers alike, since it boasts several natural attractions and a well-structured network of trails. The celebrated Appalachian Trail runs through the region from west to east, leading hikers to the most beautiful summits in this part of the country.

 Practical Information

Franconia Notch State Park, Franconia, New Hampshire 03580, ☎ (603) 745-8391 or 823-5563.

 Exploring

Go swimming in **Echo Lake** *($2.50; ☎ 603-823-5563)*. Gorgeous beach, canoe rentals, fishing, etc.

Check out the Old Man of the Mountain, a giant human face carved by the elements into Cannon Mountain. A small trail leads from Profile Lake and offers different views of this 12-m-by-8-m face. Set about 360 m above the lake, this curious formation was first noticed in 1805.

Take the **Aerial Tramway** *($8 return, $6 one-way, ☎ 603-823-5563)* to the top of Cannon Mountain (1,274 m), which offers some magnificent views of the valley and the Franconia Range. There are hiking trails as well. Cannon Mountain takes its name from the cannon-shaped boulder on its summit, which can be seen from the valley.

Visit the **New England Ski Museum**, located right beside the Aerial Tramway *(free admission;* ☎ *603-823-7177)*. Equipment, clothing, photographs, videos and artwork related to the history of downhill and cross-country skiing are on display.

Visit **The Basin** *(*☎ *603-745-8391)*, a chasm 5 m deep and 10 m in diametre, located along little Route 3, just north of The Flume.

Go cycling in the valley, on the Recreational Trail (bike rentals available at Cannon Mountain).

Watch rock-climbers scale the imposing rock face of Cannon Mountain. There are many difficult and spectacular routes up this gigantic wall of rock.

 Accommodations

■ **Camping**

Lafayette Campground, Franconia Notch State Park, ☎ (603) 823-9513.

 Short Hikes

■ **Artists Bluff and Bald Mountain**

Level of difficulty:	
Total distance:	*2.4 km loop*
Time:	*1 h 15 min*
Change in altitude:	*120 m*
Starting point:	*parking lot at Echo Lake, on Route 18, right near Interstate 93*

This short, easy trail enables hikers to enjoy some wonderful views of Franconia Notch without having to walk for hours.

Starting at the Echo Lake parking lot, cross Route 18 and head for Interstate 93. The trail starts on the left and climbs straight up to a small intersection, which you'll reach in a few minutes. The short trail on the right leads to a superb scenic viewpoint known as Artists Bluff, since so many artists go there to paint the valley.

Cannon Mountain, scored with ski trails, cuts an imposing figure up ahead, to the right. The mountain's first tramway was built in 1938. The present one (Tram 2), constructed in 1980, takes 5 min to climb the 615 m to the top of the mountain. Each car can carry 80 passengers. Mount Lafayette, the highest peak in Franconia Notch (1,603 m), dominates the landscape to the left.

Go back to the intersection and turn right on the trail that climbs up into the forest. After reaching a small viewpoint, it heads down to an old road. Turn right onto the trail that leads up to the top of Bald Mountain, which offers a view of the village of Franconia and Cannon Mountain.

Head back down to the intersection and turn right on the old road, which leads to Route 18. When you reach the highway, turn left and walk back down to the Echo Lake parking lot. Relaxing on the beach or taking a dip in the lake are both excellent ways to top off the day.

■ Mounts Lincoln and Lafayette

Level of difficulty:	⌃⌃⌃
Total distance:	*14.5 km loop*
Time:	*7 h 30 min*
Change in altitude:	*1,143 m*
Starting point:	*parking lot beside the Visitor Center at Lafayette Campground (if you're coming from the south, there is another parking lot on the east side of Interstate 93).*

This loop takes hikers to the top of two magnificent mountains in Franconia Notch. As Mount Lincoln (1,551 m) and Mount Lafayette (1,603 m) are only 2.7 km apart, it would be a shame not to include both in the same excursion—especially since the Franconia Ridge Trail, which runs between them, is one of the most spectacular in all of New England. To complete the loop, you'll use the Falling Waters, Franconia Ridge and Greenleaf Trails, and the Old Bridle Path.

Starting at the parking lot of the Visitor Center, take the trail that runs under Interstate 93 to the parking lot on the east side of the highway. For the first 0.4 km or so, the Falling Waters Trail overlaps the Old

Bridle Path. When you reach the little bridge over Walker Creek, turn right on the Falling Waters Trail, which climbs gently up to Dry Brook (1.1 km). Despite its name, this brook is anything but dry in the spring. The trail gets steeper on its way across the rocks in the stream, near the pool.

Farther along, the path runs near the Stairs and Swiftwater Falls and intersects with a small forest road, no longer in use. Shortly after the Cloudland Falls, you'll come to a scenic viewpoint overlooking the valley, followed by another small road a little higher. The trail then leads left, climbing up the ridge to a small intersection where a secondary trail branches off to a magnificent scenic viewpoint (Shining Rock). Still farther, the main trail intersects with the Franconia Ridge Trail (5.2 km). The vegetation is particularly fragile in this area, which lies in an alpine-arctic zone.

The Franconia Ridge Trail is located at the top of a secondary mountain known as Little Haystack (1,475 m). Head left, to the north. This ridge is one of the most spectacular in the region and makes for an unforgettable hike. Because it is so exposed, however, it can be dangerous in bad weather. This path overlaps the Appalachian Trail up to the top of the mountain.

The ridge is very narrow in places. The trail leads to the summit of Mount Lincoln (6.3 km; 1,551 m), which offers an excellent view in every direction. The trail leads down the north side of the mountain and follows the Franconia Ridge for over 1.5 km, to the top of Mount Lafayette (8 km). This last mountain (1,603 m), formerly known as Great Haystack, was renamed after the Marquis de Lafayette, who played an important role in the American Revolution.

From Mount Lafayette, turn left onto the Greenleaf Trail, which heads down toward the valley to the Greenleaf Hut (9.8 km), which can accommodate up to 48 hikers. At this point, turn left on the Old Bridle Path, which continues downhill, back to the starting point of the hike, affording some lovely views along the way. There are a few steep sections, especially at the beginning. When you reach the intersection you passed at the very beginning of the hike (Falling Waters Trail), turn right and continue to the parking lot of the Visitor Center (14.5 km).

■ **Mounts Flume and Liberty**

Level of difficulty:	⛰ ⛰ ⛰
Total distance:	*16 km loop*
Time:	*8 h*
Change in altitude:	*1,026 m*
Starting point:	*parking lot for the Whitehouse Trail, just north (about 400 m) of the Flume Visitor Center.*

Mount Flume (1,319 m) and Mount Liberty (1,359 m) are the two major mountains in the southern part of the Franconia Range. To complete this loop, you'll take the Whitehouse, Flume Slide, Franconia Ridge and Liberty Spring trails. The last-mentioned overlaps with the Appalachian Trail.

The parking lot of the Flume Visitor Center, immediately to the south, offers a splendid view of both mountains, especially Mount Flume, which rises up proudly, its steep and rocky west face clearly visible. This view offers a foretaste of the spectacular scene that awaits you at the summit of the mountain.

From the parking lot, head north on the Whitehouse Trail, which runs parallel to the Recreational Trail, a bike path leading through Franconia Notch. Near the little bridge across the Pemigewasset River, you'll pass the Cascade Brook Trail on your left. Shortly after, turn right onto the Liberty Spring Trail (1.3 km).

The Liberty Spring Trail heads northward, then veers east. After passing an old road, you'll come to an intersection (2.3 km). Head right on the Flume Slide Trail, which climbs gently uphill at first, crossing a number of streams along the way, including Flume Creek, whose shores it follows. These first 4 km are relatively easy, but the trail becomes steeper and more difficult starting at the base of the rock face (6.5 km) known as the Slide, in reference to the rock slides that have occurred here.

Climbing up these rocks can be quite difficult when they're wet. This part of the trail covers a little over a kilometre, affording a view of the valley now and again. At the top of the rock face, the trail leads left to the Franconia Ridge Trail (7.6 km). Turn left on the latter, which will quickly take you to the top of Mount Flume (1,319 m), where you'll enjoy a magnificent 360° view of the region. A number of mountains—Liberty, Lincoln, Lafayette, Cannon and Kinsman—stand out to the north and the west.

Mount Flume and Mount Liberty are 1.8 km apart (if it is getting late or the weather is bad, it is best to retrace your steps at this point). The Franconia Ridge Trail heads down Mount Flume, then follows the ridge and leads up Mount Liberty (9.6 km). At the top (1,359 m), you'll enjoy an outstanding view of Franconia Notch.

From the top of Mount Liberty, continue north on the Franconia Ridge Trail until it intersects with the Liberty Spring Trail (10.1 km). Turn left on the latter, which heads down into the valley, overlapping the Appalachian Trail. It leads first to the Liberty Spring Campsite (10.6 km), then to the intersection (13.8 km) you passed at the beginning of the hike (Flume Slide Trail). Farther down, it links up with the Whitehouse Trail (14.7 km), which leads to the parking lot.

■ The Flume

Level of difficulty:	⛰
Total distance:	*3.2 km loop*
Time:	*1 h 15 min*
Change in altitude:	*120 m*
Starting point:	*Flume Visitor Center parking lot (☎ 603-745-8391, adults $6, children 6-12 $3).*

The Flume is a small, narrow, 240-m long gorge. Located alongside Flume Brook, which flows down from Mounts Liberty and Flume, it was discovered in 1808. Wooden footbridges were built so that visitors could explore the inside of the gorge, which quickly became one of the region's most popular attractions. The trail is short (you don't even have to make the whole trip) and studded with geological formations, making it an especially big hit with children.

The Visitor Center contains a cafeteria, a souvenir shop and an exhibition area. It also displays old photographs of the region and a superb yellow Concord Coach, which was built in 1874 and wasn't retired until 1911. These coaches, which were drawn by four horses, were built between 1826 and 1900 in the little town of Concord, New Hampshire.

At the counter, make sure to pick up a free copy of the leaflet on the trail, which provides information about the natural formations you'll encounter along the way. The trail starts behind the Visitor Center, leads to a big boulder deposited here during the ice age, then heads down to the covered bridge across the Pemigewasset River.

Right nearby lies Boulder Cabin, where the bus stops. You can hear Flume Brook, and you'll see a large slab of rock polished by the flowing water. Next, you'll enter the narrow gorge, which extends 240 m. The little falls and the flow of water vary according to the season. Upstream, you'll find the Avalanche Falls, which plunge 14 m.

From the falls, the trail leads north, where hikers can admire the Liberty and Cascade Gorges, the Sentinel Pine covered bridge and a large pool on the Pemigewasset River. The path then heads back to the starting point, passing alongside a number of large boulders on the way.

■ **Mount Pemigewasset**

Level of difficulty:	
Total distance:	*5.8 km*
Time:	*2 h 30 min*
Change in altitude:	*356 m*
Starting point:	*Flume Visitor Centre parking lot.*

Mount Pemigewasset was named after the river that flows through the valley. Pemigewasset is an Abenaki word meaning "fast current". At the top of the mountain, there is a rock face that looks like the head of a native, aptly named the Indian Head. This hike through the area south of Franconia Notch will take you to the top of a small mountain, which offers some breathtaking views of the valley and the loftier peaks.

Starting at the Flume Visitor Center parking lot, follow the Recreational Trail bike path for a few metres, then turn left on the Mount Pemigewasset Trail. The trail passes under Route 3 and Interstate 93, then leads up into the woods, crossing a number of little streams along the way.

Shortly after intersecting with the Indian Head Trail, the path gets steeper on its way to the top of Mount Pemigewasset (2.9 km). The view from the summit (779 m) embraces the valley and the neighbouring peaks, particularly the Franconia Range (Mounts Flume, Liberty, Lincoln and Lafayette). Return by the same trail.

Kancamagus Highway

Tourists and hikers alike will find numerous points of interest along magnificent Route 112, which links the villages of Lincoln and Conway. This occasionally winding road stretches 56 km and climbs to an altitude of 900 m on its way through the Kancamagus Pass (1,136 m). "Kancamagus", which means "he who is courageous or intrepid", was the name of a local native chief reputed to have acted as a mediator between natives and whites in the late 17th century.

This road was completed in 1959 and has been attracting nature lovers ever since. A number of scenic viewpoints and picnic areas have been laid out alongside it, as well as about a dozen parking lots, which serve as the starting point for various hiking trails.

 Practical Information

Visitor Information Centers (Saco Ranger District): In Conway, on Route 112, right near Route 16. Open every day from 8am to 4:30pm. All different kinds of information, maps, books, brochures, etc., ☎ (603) 447-5448.

 Accommodations

■ **Camping**

There are six campgrounds along the Kancamagus Highway, all part of the White Mountain National Forest: Hancock, Big Rock, Passaconaway, Jigger Johnson, Blackberry Crossing and Covered Bridge. Reservations are only accepted at the Covered Bridge Campground (☎ 800-280-CAMP).

Short Hikes

■ **Sabbaday Falls**

Level of difficulty:	
Total distance:	*1.2 km*
Time:	*30 min*
Change in altitude:	*30 m*
Starting point:	*Sabbaday Falls Picnic Area, on the south side of the Kancamagus Highway, 30 km from Lincoln and 26 km from Conway.*

The short, easy, wide and well-maintained Sabbaday Brook Trail climbs up toward Mount Tripyramid. After 500 m, a small secondary trail branches off to the left, leading to the little pool at the base of the Sabbaday Falls, which are framed by a small gorge, providing a good place to relax for a bit. The path runs alongside the falls then heads back to the main trail. Turn right to return to the parking lot.

■ **The Russell-Colbath Historic Site**

Level of difficulty:	
Total distance:	*800 m loop*
Length:	*15 min*
Change in altitude:	*nil*
Starting point:	*parking lot of the Rail'n River/Russell-Colbath Historic House, on the north side of Kancamagus Highway, 35 km from Lincoln and 20 km from Conway.*

A quick stop at this historic site will enable you to learn more about this mountainous region's past and stretch your legs on a short hike.

The little wooden house was built in 1832 by Thomas Russell and his son Amzi. Russell (1768-1853) was born in Massachusetts, but his parents settled in Conway in 1772. He later spent many years in Bartlett. His son Amzi moved into this house with his wife Eliza, and they subsequently had five children. Amzi died in 1879.

By 1887, Amzi's and Eliza's daughter Ruth Priscilla and her husband Thomas Alden Colbath were living here. One day, in 1891, Thomas left the house, saying he would be back soon. When he didn't return, Ruth put a lamp in the window so he'd be able to see the house at night, and she continued to do so for 39 years! Nothing came of it, however, and in 1930, she fell sick and died at the hospital in North Conway.

Three years later, in 1933, 42 years after setting out on his little stroll, Thomas Alden Colbath resurfaced in the area. Supposedly, he was somewhat confused and had no explanation for his incredible disappearance. He claimed to have been living in California, Cuba and Panama in the interim.

Right beside the house, there is a little cemetery containing the graves of most of the Russell family; in front, Mount Passaconaway (1,238 m) rises up in the distance.

A small nature trail leads from the parking lot to the Swift River. This little loop, which is less that 1 km long, is presently being spruced up and should be reopened soon. It runs through a lovely forest containing a large variety of trees.

■ Champney Falls

Level of Difficulty:	
Total distance:	*5.6 km*
Time:	*2 h*
Change in altitude:	*210 m*
Starting point:	*parking lot on the south side of Kancamagus Highway, 37 km from Lincoln and 18.5 km from Conway.*

This trail is best hiked in springtime, as the falls slow down to just a trickle in summer.

The Champney Falls Trail leads to the top of Three Sisters Mountain (1,015 m) and Mount Chocorua (1,060 m) via the Middle Sister and Piper Trails. It climbs steadily but there are no difficult sections. After crossing Twin Brook, it follows an old forest road. At the intersection (2.2 km), turn left on the little trail leading to the falls.

The falls were named after artist Benjamin Champney (1817-1907). The trail makes a small loop back to the main trail (2.9 km). Turn right to return to the parking lot (5.6 km).

■ **Boulder Loop Trail**

Level of difficulty:
Total distance: *5 km loop*
Time: *2 h 30 min*
Change in altitude: *275 m*
Starting point: *Boulder Loop Trail parking lot. Take Dugway Road, which branches off the north side of the Kancamagus Highway 44 km from Lincoln and 12 km from Conway. Cross the marvelous little covered bridge and continue to the Boulder Loop Trail parking lot. The trail is located right beside the Covered Bridge Campground.*

This is a self-guided trail, so make sure to pick up the little leaflet explaining the area's distinctive natural features, available at the beginning of the trail and at the Visitor Information Centers in Conway (see above).

The trail has 8 stops covering subjects such as geological history, rock formations, erosion, rivers and streams, moss, various species of trees and logging. Hikers also get to enjoy some pretty views, especially from the top of the rocky ledge overhanging the cliffs. The path leading there starts at the intersection (2.4 km) halfway around the loop.

Crawford Notch

Crawford Notch lies southwest of Mount Washington, along Route 302, which links Twin Mountain to Bartlett. This mountain pass, formed by a drifting icecap, is part of Crawford Notch State Park. It is about 10 km long and closely hemmed in by big, steep-faced mountains.

This long, narrow mountain pass was discovered by Timothy Nash while he was out hunting in 1771. It is said that Governor John Wentworth promised land to anyone who succeeded in making it through the pass on horseback. This took several attemps, as horses had to be lowered down the cliffs with ropes. Shortly after, a small road was laid, making it possible to cross the mountains and colonize the northern part of the state.

Because the cliffs are so steep in this area, the local inhabitants had to cope with landslides. The year 1826 went down in local history when a fierce storm hit the region, triggering several landslides. Samuel Willey and his family, who lived right in the middle of Crawford Notch, were killed by falling debris; curiously enough, however, their house was not buried. Apparently, upon hearing the raging storm, the family went outside, thus sealing their fate. Only a few of the bodies were found. This mysterious tragedy soon became a legend, generating all sorts of theories as to what happened.

You can learn more about this tragic tale at the Willey House Historic Site. The mountain to the west of the pass, behind the site, was named Mount Willey (1,311 m) in honour of the family. A number of other peaks tower over this unique landscape: Mounts Willard (866 m), Avalon (1,045 m), Field (1,319 m) and Tom (1,234 m) form the west ridge of the pass, Mounts Webster (1,192 m) and Jackson (1,235 m) the east.

There are a number of waterfalls in this narrow pass. The Silver and Flume Falls, which lie to the north, near Saco Lake, are magnificent in springtime. There is a small parking lot along Route 302, where you can stop and admire them. Visiting the Kedron Flume, Ripley Falls and Arethusa Falls requires a little more effort (see below).

❓ Practical Information

Crawford Notch State Park: Information office at the Willey House Historic Site, on Route 302 *(☎ 603-374-2272)*.

Crawford Depot Information Center (AMC): Information office on Route 302, in the old train station near Saco Lake.

Accommodations

■ Camping

Dry River Campground: Located south of the valley, along Route 302, 19 km from Bartlett *(☎ 603-374-2272)*.

Short Hikes

■ The Waterfalls of Crawford Notch

Keep in mind that all the following waterfalls are most spectacular in the springtime, when the water is high.

The **Kedron Flume** is located right behind the Willey House Historic Site. The Kedron Flume Trail starts at the picnic area next to the buildings (2.5 km return).

Farther south, the trail to the **Ripley Falls** starts near the railroad tracks, at the Willey House Station. The Ripley Falls Trail (1.6 km return) climbs quickly up to the falls, which are over 30 m high.

The **Arethusa Falls**, a little more to the south, plunge 60 m, making them the highest falls in the state of New Hampshire. The Arethusa Falls Trail (4.2 km return) starts at the Arethusa Falls parking lot, near the railroad tracks, 5.5 km south of the Willey House Historic Site, and leads straight up to the falls.

■ Mount Willard

Level of difficulty:	
Total distance:	*5.2 km*
Time:	*2 h*
Change in altitude:	*285 m*
Starting point:	*Crawford Depot parking lot.*

Among the smaller peaks that are easy to scale, Mount Willard (866 km) is said to offer the most beautiful view of all the White Mountains.

The Mount Willard Trail starts on the other side of the railroad tracks, behind Crawford Depot, and overlaps with the Avalon Trail for a few metres. Turn left at the intersection. The trail then climbs straight up to the top of Mount Willard, running alongside an old forest road (1.2 km) part of the way. Near the summit, a small secondary trail leads to a lovely scenic viewpoint. The main trail ends just east of the summit (2.6 km).

Your efforts will be well rewarded by a truly outstanding view of the valley and a good part of the western portion of the White Mountains, as far as famous Mount Washington. Mounts Avalon (1,045 m) and Field (1,319 m) rise up behind Mount Willard, to the west. These two peaks, linked by the Avalon Trail, also offer magnificent views of the region. Return by the same trail.

■ **Mount Crawford**

Level of difficulty:	
Total distance:	*8 km*
Time:	*4 h 30 min*
Change in altitude:	*640 m*
Starting point:	*the Davis Path parking lot, along Route 302, 9 km south of the Willey House Historic Site, opposite the Notchland Inn.*

The trail leading to Mount Crawford (954 m) is known as the Davis Path. Nathaniel Davis cleared it in 1844 in order to access Mount Washington from the south.

From the parking lot, the trail follows a little road alongside the Saco River. After crossing the river on a small suspension bridge called Bemis Bridge, it becomes quite steep. Mr. Davis's numerous efforts to make the trail safer as it zigzags up the ridge have survived to this day. After reaching a viewpoint overlooking Crawford Notch, you'll come to an intersection (3.5 km).

Head left on the trail leading to the top of Mount Crawford (4 km). By walking around on the summit, you can take in views in all directions. Crawford Notch lies below, while the silhouettes of lofty mountains stand out against the horizon. Return by the same trail.

Mount Washington Region

Mount Washington (1,917 m) is the highest and most celebrated mountain east of the Mississippi and north of North Carolina. Containing no fewer than ten summits, this small region is truly awesome, offering something for everyone from the inexperienced beginner to the serious climber.

Each of the ten summits in the Presidential Range is named after a former American president: Madison, Adams, Jefferson, Washington, Clay, Monroe, Franklin, Clinton, Jackson, and Eisenhower. Each summit is located above the timberline and offers a commanding view of the White Mountains.

Because of its geographical location, Mount Washington's climate is similar to Labrador's. The most violent winds ever registered, 369 km/hr, were recorded at the summit of Mount Washington in 1934. The summit is enshrouded in clouds 300 days of the year, so do not venture too high in bad weather. In fact, the phenomenon of altitude versus temperature is well demonstrated in the White Mountains. Climbing 300 m here is like heading 370 km north. Reaching the summit of Mount Washington from Pinkham Notch which is a change in altitude of 1,306 m, is like finding yourself 1,600 km farther north, all the way in Kuujjuaq, Northern Quebec! It is therefore not surprising that the average temperature at the summit of Mount Washington in July is 9.4°C!

The Algonquins originally called Mount Washington *Agiocochook*, which means "the mountain on this side". The Italian explorer Verrazano was the first European to lay eyes on the White Mountains during an expedition in 1524. The first known ascent was in 1642, by Darby Field and two Abenakis who, according to records, did not go all the way to the summit for fear they would anger their Gods.

The presence of various buildings on the mountain has somewhat marred the impression that you are exploring uncharted territory. The first building was the weather station, constructed in 1870. Others soon followed, like the Yankee Building, in 1941, which houses radio and television transmitters, and the Stage Office, in 1908, used for the maintenance of the Auto Road. This road leads cars up to the summit, but it is quite expensive. The main building houses a restaurant, souvenir shop, toilets, telephones, a post office, and the Mount Washington Museum and observatory. It is open from mid-May to mid-October.

Finding Your Way Around

The closest major highway to Mount Washington is Interstate 93, in the area east of St. Johnsbury and the intersection between Interstates 91 and 93.

To reach the starting points at Pinkham Notch, Lowe's Store, Valley Way Parking, 19 Mile Brook Parking, Glen House, Dolly Copp Campground and Gorham Kelley's Supermarket take Exit 42 from Interstate 93 to Route 302 East. Continue along 302 East to the intersection with Route 116. Follow 116 North to Whitefield. Be careful here because the signs for Routes 116 and 3 overlap. Continue on 116 North to Route 2 East (Lowe's Store, Valley Way Parking, and Gorham Kelley's Supermarket starting points are on this road) all the way to Gorham. From there take Route 16 South to reach the Dolly Copp Campground, Glen House, 19 Mile Brook Parking and Pinkham Notch starting points.

To reach the starting points at Crawford Depot, Webster Cliff and Ammonoosuc Ravine Trail, take Interstate 93 East to Exit 40, then follow Route 302 East. At Fabyan take Base Road to the railroad parking lot where you will find the beginning of the Ammonoosuc Ravine Trail. To reach Crawford Depot and Webster Cliff Trail continue along Route 302. Both sites are well indicated.

■ **Parking**

There is parking available at the following locations: Pinkham Notch, Lowe's Store, Valley Way Parking, 19 Mile Brook Parking, Dolly Copp Campground (fee), Crawford Depot, and Marshfield Base Station (railroad starting point).

? **Practical Information**

■ **Camping Stores**

International Mountain Equipment (IME)
Main Street
North Conway
☎ (603) 356-6316

Eastern Mountain Sports (EMS)
Main Street
North Conway
☎ (603) 356-5433

■ **Hiking Clubs**

Appalachian Mountain Club
Pinkham Notch Camp,
Route 16,
Gorham, NH 03581
☎ 603-466-3994, 466-2721

or

AMC
5 Joy Street
Boston, Massachusetts, 02108
☎ (617) 523-0636

The Appalachian Mountain Club (AMC) was founded in 1876. It is very visible in New England, particularly where forest, flora and fauna conservation are concerned. The club also manages and maintains many shelters. As publisher of several excellent hiking guides and books, the club has become the official reference on this subject. The *AMC White Mountain Guide*, which first appeared in 1907, is just one example. This 600-page guide boasts many maps and is in its 25th edition (1992). With over 60,000 members, the AMC is well informed.

■ Police

New Hampshire State Police
Troop F,
Route 302,
Twin Mountain, NH
☎ 603-846-5500 or 1-800-852-3411

 Tourist Information

North Conway
☎ 603-356-3961 or 1-800-367-3364

■ Public Transportation

The Appalachian Mountain Club (AMC) has organized a fully functioning public transportation system permitting visitors to explore the whole Mount Washington area, all the way to Mount Lafayette. There are three mini-bus circuits: the Pinkham AM and PM Shuttles, the Appalachian AM Shuttle, and the Crawford AM and PM shuttles. You can transfer from one shuttle to another at Crawford Depot Jct., between Routes 302 and 115.

The transport system is in operation from the beginning of June to the beginning of September. It is best to reserve a seat ahead of time *(☎ 603-466-2727, or in person at Pinkham Notch or AMC lodges)*.

 Exploring

Ride to the summit of Mount Washington aboard the **Mount Washington Cog Railway** *($35 return;* ☎ *603-846-5404)*, which is accessible by Route 302 in Bretton Woods. The spectacular return trip (37% incline) takes three hours.

You can also reach the summit by car, via the **Mount Washington Auto Road** *($15 for a car and driver, $6 for adult passengers, $4 for children,* ☎ *603-466-3988)*. The starting point is on Route 16, just north of Pinkham Notch Camp. This road was constructed in 1861, and is open, weather-permitting, from mid-May to the end of October. A bicycle race has been run every year in August since 1973. This little 13-km road, the average incline of which is 12%, presents quite a challenge to courageous cyclists. If you prefer, you can participate in the run held every June since 1960.

Near Glen is the **Grand Manor Car Museum** *(☎ 603-356-9366)*, the **Heritage New Hampshire Historical Centre** *(☎ 603-383-9776)*, and **Storyland**, an exhibition for children *(☎ 603-383-4293)*.

Take a ride on the little train that follows the Saco River. With departures from North Conway, the **Conway Scenic Railroad** *(☎ 603-356-5251)* offers three spectacular tours (all return trips). The North Conway-Conway trip is 18-km long *(1 hour; adults $8, children $5.50)*, the North Conway-Bartlett trip is 34-km long *(1 hour 45 min; adults $13.50, children $8.50)* and the North Conway-Crawford Notch trip is 80 km long *(5 hours; adults $32, children $17)*.

 Accommodations

■ **Camping**

Backwoods camping is permitted in most of White Mountain National Forest (WMNF). Certain restrictions do exist, however, to avoid exploitation and destruction of the forest's natural resources. Camping and campfires are forbidden above the timberline (where the trees are less than 2 m high), less than 60 m from trails (except in designated areas) and less than a quarter mile (0.4 km) from certain roads, rivers, campsites, shelters, and lodges (except in designated areas).

Some camping areas are designated "Restricted Use Areas", meaning you need a permit to camp in the Great Gulf between June 15th and September 15th. The permit is free and available from the Androscoggin Ranger District Office in Gorham *(☎ 603-466-2713)* between May 1st and October 31st or from the Dolly Copp Campground between July 1st and Labour Day (beginning of September). Dolly Copp Campground is the only site in the Presidential Range area where trailers are permitted.

Gorham

Timberland Camping Area *(☎ 603-466-3872)*

Glen

Glen Ellis Family Campground *(☎ 603-383-9320)*
Green Meadow Camping Area *(☎ 603-383-6801)*

North Conway

Saco River Camping Area *(☎ 603-356-3360)*

■ **Shelters**

Shelter	Capacity	Access Trail
Hermit Lake Shelters	90 people	Tuckerman RavineTrail
Log Cabin	10 people	Lowe's Path
Crag Camp	14 people	near Lowe's Path
Gray Knob	12 people	near Lowe's Path
The Perch	8 people	Perch Path

Hermit Lake Shelters: located at the foot of the magnificent Tuckerman Ravine, one of the major attractions for hikers in the Presidential Range. The site also offers lean-tos capable of accommodating up to 86 people. Reservation tickets are available at Pinkham Notch on a first-come, first-served basis for $7. The tickets are non-transferable and non-refundable. Between December 1st and April 1st, ten campsites are available, able to accommodate 40 people. On high-traffic weekends like Labour Day and Easter it is recommended to arrive very early Friday to get a spot.

Services: Flush toilets, water. Absolutely no campfires are permitted so bring your campstove.

Distance from Pinkham Notch to Hermit Lake Shelters: 3.9 km.

The Log Cabin: The original structure of this shelter was built in 1890 by Dr. W. G. Nowell. It is a closed shelter which can hold 10 people *($3)*, and is located on Lowe's Path at an elevation of 1000 m. It is strictly forbidden to build campfires. Meals must be prepared on campstoves.

Services: outhouse, water (stream). No campfires permitted.

Distance from Route 2 to Log Cabin: 3.7 km.

Crag Camp: This is a small, closed shelter located on the ridge of the King Ravine. The beautiful site has a fabulous view of the surrounding valleys. The shelter can accommodate 14 people. During the months of July and August it is supervised by a caretaker who collects the fee of $7 per night. For the rest of the season the Randolph Mountain Club relies on the honour system; hikers should send the fee to the following address: Randolph Mountain Club, Randolph, N.H., 03570.

The easiest way to reach Crag Camp is by Lowe's Path. Pass in front of Log Cabin, continue to the intersection of Lowe's Path and Gray Knob Trail. After passing in front of Log Cabin continue along the same trail to Crag Camp.

Services: outhouse, water (stream), kitchen facilities in summer. Absolutely no campfires permitted.

Distance from Route 2 to Crag Camp: 5.6 km.

Gray Knob: This shelter is right next to Crag Camp but its view does not quite compare. In 1989 the shelter was burnt down and rebuilt on more solid ground because the original building was collapsing. The shelter can accommodate 12 people and is supervised year-round. The quickest way to Gray Knob is along Lowe's Path to the intersection with Gray Knob Trail. The shelter is a short distance down Gray Knob Trail.

Services: outhouse, water, kitchen facilities in summer. Absolutely no campfires permitted.

Distance from Route 2 to Gray Knob: 4.8 km.

The Perch: This is a small open shelter, with room for eight people, located on the slope of the Castles Ravine. The shortest way there is to follow Castle Trail for 2 km, then join up with the Israel Ridge Path. Cross three intersections on the Israel Ridge Path (Castle Ravine Trail, the Link and Emerald Trail) before taking Perch Path to the shelter. Close to the shelter there are four tent platforms. The shelter is not supervised but the caretaker of Gray Knob passes by frequently to collect the $3 per night fee.

Services: outhouse and water. Absolutely no campfires are permitted.

Distance between Route 2 and the Perch: 5.6 km.

■ Lodges

About 100 years ago the Appalachian Mountain Club constructed their first lodge in the Presidential Range, between the summits of Mount Madison and Mount Adams. Today a whole network of lodges exists in the White Mountains on a 90-km stretch from Lonesome Lake Hut to Carter Notch Hut.

The lodges are popular because of the comfort and security they offer. They are all located along the ridge of the Presidential Range, all within about a day's walk of each other. Using these lodges eliminates the necessity of carrying your life (sleeping bag, tent, campstove, and fuel) on your back.

It is strongly recommended that you reserve ahead of time for weekends, or for any time during the months of July and August. Reservations can be made by calling ☎ (603) 466-2727 from September to May between 9am and 4pm, or from June to August between 9am and 9pm. A deposit of $20 per person is required, Visa and Mastercard are accepted.

All of the lodges along the Presidential Range are open from the beginning of May to the beginning of September. Mizpah Spring Hut offers complete service until the beginning of October.

Current Prices:	Regular	Reduced	Child
Lodging, breakfast and supper	$55	$50	$17
Lodging, breakfast or supper	$37	$37	$14
Lodging only	$12	$12	$12

These prices are in US dollars and apply to Appalachian Mountain Club members. If you are not a member, add $7 for adults and $3 for children. The regular price is in effect Fridays and Saturdays and throughout the months of July and August. Outside of these times the reduced price applies.

Mizpah Spring Hut: This lodge, located on the southern slope of Mount Clinton at an altitude of 1,160 m, can accommodate 60 people.

Distance to reach Mizpah Hut:

- Route 302 via Crawford Path: 4.5 km, about 2 h 30 min.
- Lakes of the Clouds via Crawford Path: 6.9 km, about 2 hours.
- Route 302, via Webster Cliff Trail: 9.3 km, about 6 hours.

Lakes of the Clouds Hut: Located at 1,500 m on a small plateau between Mount Washington and Mount Monroe, this is the highest lodge in the Presidential Range, with the best panoramic view of the region. It is accessible by the Crawford Path or by the Ammonoosuc Ravine Trail and can accommodate 90 people.

Distance to reach Lakes of the Clouds Hut:

- Marshfield Base Station parking via Ammonoosuc Ravine Trail: 4 km, approximately 3 h 30 min.
- Mizpah Hut via Crawford Path: 6.9 km, about 3 hours.

Madison Springs Hut: Located between Mount Madison and Mount Adams, this lodge can accommodate 50 people. The terrain around the site is quite rough compared to the other lodges. There is, however, a spectacular view of summits to the north and south.

Distance to reach Madison Spring Hut:

- Pinkham Notch via Old Jackson Road and Madison Gulf Trail: 9.8 km, about 5 hours.
- Lakes of the Clouds via Crawford Path, Washington Summit and Gulfside Trails; 12.5 km, approximately 6 hours.
- Appalachian parking on Route 2, via Valley Way: 5.6 km, about 4 hours.

Pinkham Notch Camp: This lodge, situated at the base of Mount Washington, serves as a sort of general centre for the Appalachian Mountain Club. A few hours away from Tuckerman Ravine and Alpine Garden, it is two steps from Crystal Cascades and Glen Ellis Falls. It is the preferred starting point of hikers mainly because of the numerous hiking possibilities in the area. All types of information and facilities are available at the lodge: weather reports, a library, guides, maps, environmental information, showers, clothes dryers, etc.

Pinkham Notch is open year-round and can accommodate 106 people in 2-, 3- or 4-person rooms. The prices are the same as for the other lodges.

■ **Hotels, Motels, Inns ...**

There is an abundance of choices in the region of Mount Washington. Dozens of hotels and motels, many of them over a hundred years old, are located in the area.

North Conway

Stonehurst Manor *(Route 16, ☎ 1-800-525-9100)*: Nineteenth-century manor house. Guided hikes, mountain bikes, nature, tours, etc..

Eastman Inn *(☎ 603-356-6707 or 1-800-626-5855)*: Eighteenth-century bed and breakfast.

The 1785 Inn *(☎ 603-356-9025)*: Country inn from the 18th-century. Houses a great restaurant (seafood and grilled delights).

Maple Leaf Motel *(☎ 603-356-5388)*: well kept and affordable. Open year-round.

Merrill Farm Resort *(☎ 1-800-445-1017 or 603-447-3866)*: Located along the Saco River. Canadian money accepted at par.

Gorham

Top Notch Motor Inn *(☎ 1-800-228-5496 or 603-466-5496)*: Free tea and coffee, with a pool. Close to everything.

Mount Madison Motel *(☎ 1-800-851-1136 or 603-466-3622)*: large beds, pool, etc.

Glen

Linderhof Motor Inn *(☎ 603-383-4334)*: Bavarian-style inn with a beautiful view of the mountains.

Bernerhof Inn *(☎ 1-800-548-8007 or 603-383-4414)*: nine spectacular rooms, European-style restaurant and bar.

Conway

Mountain Valley Manor *(☎ 603-447-3988)*: Bed and breakfast in a beautiful Victorian house, with assured privacy (4 rooms).

The Darby Field Inn *(☎ 1-800-426-4147 or 603-447-2181)*: Country inn, gourmet cuisine, and view of the mountains.

 Short Hikes

■ **Boy Mountain**

Level of difficulty:	
Total distance:	*2.2 km*
Time:	*1 hour*
Change in altitude:	*209 m*

Starting point:	*Along Route 2, 2.1 km east of Route 115. The parking lot is located on the south side of the road, by the small, semicircular stone wall. The magnificent Carter-Brigman house lies across the road.*

Cross Route 2 at the little spring and walk up the lane between the house and the garage. Right behind the house, you'll find a small sign for the Boy Mountain Trail, which is maintained by the Carter-Brigman family and open to hikers.

The path is short, easy and well maintained. There are a few arrows and markers to show the way. After a few minutes, you'll reach the wooded summit of Boy Mountain (681 m). Just before, however, there is a small ledge, which offers a magnificent view of the valley and the Presidential Range. The view of these lofty peaks, from the north side, is quite unusual. Return by the same trail.

■ **Mount Starr King**

Level of difficulty:	◩◩
Total distance:	*9 km*
Time:	*4 hours*
Change in altitude:	*735 m*
Starting point:	*Starr King-Waumbek parking lot. On Route 2, in Jefferson, 5.8 km west of Route 115. Immediately opposite the entrance to the Waumbek Golf Club, head left on the little road leading up to the parking lot (it is marked by a sign); stay to the left on the way up.*

Mount Starr King is located northwest of Mount Washington. Its summit (1,191 m) offers an outstanding and unusual panoramic view of the lofty peaks of the Presidential Range.

The trail starts out by following a small road, turns left, then links back up with the road. To the right, the trail leads to some old stone foundations. You will then reach a fork; stay to the right (0.6 km) in order to climb the southwest ridge of Mount Starr King, up to the summit (4.5 km). The scenic viewpoint is about 60 m farther.

The Presidential Range is absolutely spectacular from this vantage point, which offers a perfect view of Mount Washington (1,917 m), the highest peak in the northeastern United States, as well as Mounts Clay (1,689 m), Jefferson (1,741 m), Adams (1.760 m) and Madison (1.636 m), which extend to the left. Return by the same trail.

■ Mount Adams

Air Line and Valley Way Trails

Level of difficulty:	⌃⌃⌃
Total distance:	*14.5 km loop*
Time:	*7 h 30 min*
Change in altitude:	*1,370 m*
Starting point:	*the Appalachia parking lot, located on Route 2, 8.8 km west of Gorham and 1.6 km west of Pinkham B (Dolly Copp) Road.*

Mount Adams (1,760 m) is the second highest of the White Mountains. Its huge ridge, ravines and steep summit make it a favourite with serious hikers. The trip up the north side involves a greater change in altitude than climbing to the top of Mount Washington from Pinkham Notch, so make sure to set out early in the morning if you want to take your time and make the most of the day.

This hike is a loop. You'll take the Air Line Trail up the mountain and the Valley Way Trail back down. From the Appalachia parking lot, follow the trail that leads across the railroad tracks and branches into the Air Line and Valley Way Trails. Head right on the Air Line Trail, which was cleared in 1885. At the beginning of the hike, a number of other paths intersect with the Air Line Trail, so be careful to stay on course.

The trail becomes steeper on its way to Durand Ridge, parts of which, such as the Knife Edge, are very beautiful. The view of King Ravine, to the right, is sure to make your heart beat a little faster. The Chemin des Dames leads from the Air Line Trail into the ravine. Higher up, another trail branches off to the left, leading to the Madison Hut. The main trail then leads right up to the top of the ravine, veers left, splitting off from the Gulfside Trail, and climbs all the way to the top of Mount Adams (6.9 km).

In clear weather, the view from the top of Mount Adams (1,760 m) seems infinite, embracing Mounts Washington, Jefferson, Madison and several others. To get back down the mountain, retrace your steps to the Gulfside Trail. Instead of staying on the Air Line Trail (to the left), however, take the Gulfside Trail to the Madison Hut.

At the Madison Hut, pick up the Valley Way Trail, which leads down to the Appalachia parking lot, intersecting with the Air Line Trail near the end. This trail is considered the safest route between the parking lot and Madison Hut, whether you're travelling up or down.

■ Lowe's Path Trail

Level of difficulty:	〽〽〽
Total distance:	*14.4 km*
Time:	*7 h 30 min*
Change in altitude:	*1,300 m*
Starting point:	*west of Lowe's Store on Route 2.*

Lowe's Path Trail ascends to the summit of Mount Adams (1,757 m). It was cleared in 1876, making it one of the oldest trails in the area.

The trail crosses the railroad tracks and then climbs gently crossing a few streams. Lowe's Path Trail intersects several other trails, and passes close to Log Cabin Lodge (where there is water) and Gray Knob shelter (reached via the path of the same name).

Here the trail becomes more difficult and more open. The view above the timberline stretches for miles and is spectacular. You will reach a smaller peak called Adams-4, and cross a few more trails (one of which is Gulfside Trail) before reaching the summit of Mount Adams — the second highest in New England (Mount Washington is the highest). Return by the same trail; other variations are also possible.

■ Mount Jefferson

Caps Ridge Trail

Level of difficulty:	〽〽
Total distance:	*8 km*
Time:	*4 hours*

Change in altitude:	*824 m*
Starting point:	*Jefferson Notch Road. From Route 302, in Fabyan, take Base Road, which leads to the Cog Railway Station. Before reaching the station, turn left on Jefferson Notch Road and continue for about 5 km to the beginning of the trail.*

At the beginning of the Caps Ridge Trail, you are already at an altitude of 917 m. Although the trail is relatively short, some parts of it are very difficult and very steep. It is also poorly sheltered from the elements. Many hikers hoping to enjoy a short outing have had to turn back for this very reason. Not only does rain make the rock very slippery, but the winds in this region can be unbelievable.

After crossing a humid zone, the trail immediately starts climbing up the ridge. You'll come to a scenic viewpoint (1.6 km), from which you can contemplate both Mount Jefferson and the ridge. You'll also see a number of small chasms formed during the ice age. A little farther along, the Link Trail intersects with the Caps Ridge Trail from the left. The next part of the Caps Ridge Trail is steeper and affords some lovely views.

From the Lowest Cap (2.4 km) to the summit, the trail is completely exposed. After the Upper Cap (1,472 m), the trail continues climbing. Once you reach the intersection with the Cornice Trail (3.4 km), you only have 650 m to go to reach the top of Mount Jefferson (4 km). The summit (1,741 m) is made up of three rocky crests, all offering equally spectacular views of the region. Return by the same trail.

Variation: From the top of Mount Jefferson, make a loop by heading north on the Castle Trail then turning left on the Link Trail. This will take you back to the Caps Ridge Trail; turn right to return to the starting point. This 10.5 km loop makes for a very arduous hike.

Castle Trail

Level of difficulty:	⌂⌂⌂
Total distance:	*16.2 km*
Time:	*8 hours*
Change in altitude:	*1,310 m*
Starting point:	*Route 2, 1.6 km west of Lowe's Store.*

This trail, which follows Castellated Ridge, provides a striking view of the Castle Ravine and of Mount Jefferson. The trail narrows as it approaches the tower shaped rocks of Castle Ridge. The panoramic view of the region from the top of these rocks makes it worth the climb. Many precipitous boulders block the trail leading to the slopes of Mount Jefferson.

■ Mount Eisenhower

Level of difficulty:	⚠ ⚠
Total distance:	*10.6 km*
Time:	*5 hours*
Change in altitude:	*830 m*
Starting point:	*Parking lot on Mount Clinton Road, 3.7 km north of Route 302. The road starts just north of Crawford Depot. You can also reach it via Base Road, which leads to the Cog Railway.*

This superb trail, known as Edmands Path, enables hikers to climb to the top of Mount Eisenhower without expending a tremendous amount of effort. Created by J. Rayner Edmands in 1909, it soon became a favourite with local hikers. The parking lot is therefore rarely empty. Although the trail is not very difficult, one part near the summit is exposed and should be avoided if a storm breaks out.

The first part of the trail leads across the Abenaki Stream (0.6 km), then follows an old road through the forest. Veering off to the left, it gets steeper on its way up the western ridge of the mountain. It then leads north, crossing a small stream, and skirts round the summit of Mount Eisenhower.

Farther up, the trail intersects with Crawford Path and the Mount Eisenhower Loop (4.9 km). Head right on the latter, which leads to the top of the mountain (5.3 km). Fragile alpine plants grow on the summit (1,451 m), which is shaped like a giant dome and offers a 360° view of the region. Return by the same trail.

■ **Slide Peak**

Glen Boulder Trail

Level of difficulty:	⌃⌃
Total distance:	*8 km*
Time:	*4 h 30 min*
Change in altitude:	*850 m*
Starting point:	*Glen Ellis parking lot, on Route 16, just south of Pinkham Notch.*

This trail leads to the summit of Slide Peak (1,457 m). The trail rises gradually and fairly quickly and provides good views of Wildcat Mountain and Pinkham Notch.

The trail then becomes quite steep and crosses first a cross-country ski trail and then a stream. Above the timberline the trail opens onto a gigantic rock overhang from which the view of the valley is breathtaking.

Further along the trail is a spring, located just below and only a few minutes from Slide Peak. Return by the same trail.

■ **Mount Jackson**

Webster-Jackson Trail

Level of difficulty:	⌃
Total distance:	*8.6 km*
Time:	*4 h 30 min*
Change in altitude:	*652 m*
Starting point:	*on Route 302, just south of Crawford Depot.*

There are a few trails to the summit of Mount Jackson, the Webster-Jackson Trial being the main one. After 2.2 km the trail splits. Follow the left fork up to the crest of Mount Jackson (1,228 m) for a staggering view.

Variation: From the top of Mount Jackson it is possible to pick up the Webster Cliff Trail leading to the summit of Mount Webster. From there follow the Webster-Jackson Trail to form a loop (this adds just 1.6 km to the total distance).

■ **Pine Mountain**

Ledge Trail

Level of difficulty:	⌂
Total distance:	*5.2 km*
Time:	*2 hours*
Change in altitude:	*228 m*
Starting point:	*on Dolly Copp Road, between Routes 16 and 2.*

The private road to the peak of Pine Mountain can be walked but not driven.

The road, after a short distance, links up with Ledge Trail, which leads to the top of Pine Mountain (728 m). There are many exceptional views from this summit.

It is possible to walk in a loop by following the Tractor Road on the way back.

■ **Mount Washington**

Tuckerman Ravine Trail

Level of difficulty:	⌂ ⌂ ⌂
Total distance:	*13.5 km*
Time:	*7 hours*
Change in altitude:	*1,306 m*
Starting point:	*Pinkham Notch.*

Tuckerman Ravine Trail is the most popular trail in the Presidential Range. Thousands of hikers and skiers use it each year to get to Hermit Lake to admire the glacial wonders of Tuckerman Ravine. In springtime avid skiers hit the steep slopes which often remain covered with snow well into the month of June.

This trail is most interesting at Hermit Lake. Between Pinkham Notch and Hermit Lake it has no particular attraction except Crystal Cascades.

Hermit Lake is an important crossroads to Mount Washington since it provides access to some of the most beautiful trails of the presidential range. The site is an ideal base camp from which to explore new trails each day.

Past the shelter, the trail becomes progressively steeper, but it is very well groomed. The trail alongside the ravine is quite a thrill, especially for those unaccustomed to wide open space. At the top follow the directions for reaching the summit of Mount Washington. The rest of the hike is over rocky terrain, some of which is covered with a thin layer of moss, so be careful in wet weather.

Lion Head Trail

Level of difficulty:	
Total distance:	*5 km*
Time:	*2 h 45 min*
Change in altitude:	*786 m*
Starting point:	*Just before Hermit Lake Shelter.*

This trail runs along the northern edge of Tuckerman Ravine. It rises rapidly after splitting off from the trail that leads to Hermit Lake. After the steep parts have been conquered, and you find yourself on the ridge, the plunging view of the ravine is literally breathtaking. A bit further along, Alpine Garden captures the beauty and variety of alpine flora. Along the ridge winds can become quite violent, so take care.

To reach the top of Mount Washington by Lion Head Trail continue straight, following the signs leading to the summit. Be careful not to follow the Tuckerman Ravine Trail when leaving Alpine Garden.

Huntington Ravine Trail

Level of difficulty:	
Total distance:	*12.8 km*
Time:	*8 hours*
Change in altitude:	*1,306 m*
Starting point:	*Pinkham Notch.*

Huntington Ravine Trail is the most difficult in the White Mountains region. Do not attempt it if you are just starting out or if you are uncomfortable with steep trails. This trail is even more arduous if it is wet or icy. It is not recommended as a route down.

For the experienced hiker Huntington Ravine Trail presents an interesting challenge. It is so steep in certain areas that proper climbing and hand-hold techniques may be required. This trail should have thrill rating, at times you may feel like you are scaling actual rock faces!

Once at the top you can either continue to the summit of Mount Washington, or pass through Alpine Garden and descend by either Lion Head Trail or Tuckerman Ravine Trail.

■ Boott Spur Trail

Level of difficulty:	⛰⛰⛰
Total distance:	*17.2 km*
Time:	*8 hours*
Change in altitude:	*786 m*
Starting point:	*Pinkham Notch or Hermit Lake by the Boott Spur Link.*

Boott Spur is the main ridge on the south side of Mount Washington. It offers countless beautiful views of the entire Presidential Range. Mount Washington's first climbers reached its summit along this trail.

From Pinkham Notch the trail is a little tricky to find. Continue straight at the turn-off following Crystal Cascades. After passing the John Sherburne Ski Trail you should find yourself on the trail.

To reach Boott Spur from Hermit Lake Shelter, head back down to the junction of Lion Head Trail, Boott Spur Link, and Tuckerman Ravine Trail. From there follow Boott Spur Link, a very steep trail leading to the Boott Spur ridge.

From the junction to the summit of Boott Spur the views of Tuckerman Ravine, Lion Head, and Alpine Garden are spectacular. The trail ends at the intersection with Davis Path. To continue up to the crest of Mount Washington follow the right-hand trail joining up with Crawford Path. From there follow the signs to the summit.

■ **Alpine Garden Trail**

Level of difficulty:	⛰
Total distance:	*1.6 km*
Time:	*20 min*
Change in altitude:	*30 m*
Starting point:	*from the summit of Huntington Ravine or Lion Head Ridge.*

This small plateau between Huntington Ravine and Tuckerman Ravine is a bounty of New England's alpine flora. June is the time to see the largest variety of blooming flowers. The most common is the white Diapensia, which has five white petals. The AMC publishes two guides to help you identify flower species, *Field Guide to Mountain Flowers of New England* and *At Timberline: A Nature Guide to the Mountains of the Northeast.*

■ **Ammonoosuc Ravine Trail**

Level of difficulty:	⛰
Total distance:	*12.4 km*
Time:	*7 hours*
Change in altitude:	*1,192 m*
Starting point:	*Marshfield Station.*

This is the most direct route from the western side to the summit of Mount Washington. It is safe even in bad weather since it is completely protected by trees, except for the last 30 m leading up to Lakes of the Clouds Shelter.

The trail runs parallel to a refreshing stream. After about 2.2 km there is a bridge leading to a little pond at the base of a small waterfall. The trail then becomes steep (notice the change in vegetation as you gain altitude). About 100 metres further up are two very impressive waterfalls.

■ **Mount Madison**

Osgood Trail

Level of difficulty:
Total distance: *18.0 km*
Time: *7 hours*
Change in altitude: *1,178 m*
Starting point: *19 Mile Brook Parking via Great Gulf.*

The summit of Mount Madison affords the best views of the northern peaks of the Presidential Range and of the eastern slope of Mount Washington. From the parking lot, cross the road to start out on Great Gulf Trail. Follow this trail to the intersection with Osgood Trail. From there you will come upon the campsite, which is cramped and poorly maintained. The trail steepens to the timberline, at which point the hike up to the summit becomes much easier.

 Long Hikes

■ **The Great Gulf**

Level of difficulty:
Total distance: *21.4 km*
Time: *2 days*
Change in altitude: *1,306 m*
Starting Point: *Pinkham Notch.*

The valley of the Great Gulf is located between Mount Washington and the northern summits of the Presidential Range. The valley was designated a natural preservation zone in 1959 because of its numerous vistas which are among the best in New England. The first recorded explorer to lay eyes on it was Darby Field, in 1642. The name, however dates from 1823, when Ethan Allen Crawford, who lost his way in the fog, described the area as "the edge of a great gulf". A few years later the name began to appear in the literature. The Great Gulf was formed by the movement of glaciers before the last ice age.

Day One: From Pinkham Notch to the intersection of Great Gulf Trail and Wamsutta Trail.

The first day takes you into the valley of the Great Gulf. The trail is easy and pleasant. There are a number of intersections along the way so keep an eye on the signs.

Day Two: From the campsite to Pinkham Notch via the summit of Mount Washington.

If the first day was easy, the second day is to be taken more seriously. The effort will be more than rewarded by spectacular views along the trail. The most difficult part is the climb up the large rock face immediately following Spaulding Lake. Once you have reached the summit of Mount Washington the most direct route to Pinkham Notch consists of descending to Hermit Lake via Lion Head Trail, and then continuing on Tuckerman Ravine Trail to Pinkham Notch. Make sure not to push yourself on the descent since fatigue has a tendency to catch up with you on a long hike.

■ Crossing the Presidential Range

This is a classic, although not difficult, hike. Since the main part of the hike is above the timberline there is always an open view of the surrounding summits and valleys. The trail covers the base of all ten peaks of the Presidential Range.

There are two ways to do this hike. The first option is to use the AMC Lodges. This has certain advantages in terms of baggage: your backpack will be much lighter, but then again so will your wallet! The second option involves spending nights in shelters. This option requires more energy because of the extra equipment that must be carried to make the hiker self-sufficient.

First Option

Level of difficulty:	🏔🏔
Total distance:	*29 km*
Time:	*3 days*
Change in altitude:	*1,306 m*
Starting point:	*Crawford Depot (Route 302) at Appalachia Parking (Route 2).*

Day One: (11 km) from the Crawford Depot parking lot to Lakes of the Clouds via Crawford Path. This path passes Mounts Pierce (1,314 m), Eisenhower (1,451 m), Franklin (1,525 m) and Monroe (1,614 m).

Day Two: (11.9 km) from Lakes of the Clouds to Madison Hut. This day leads along an exposed ridge of the Presidential Range and allows you to climb Mounts Washington (1,917 m), Clay (1,689 m), Jefferson (1,714 m), Adams (1,760 m) and Madison (1,636 m), or to circumvent them on the Gulfside Trail.

Day Three: (6.1 km) from Madison Hut to Appalachia Parking. Several trails lead down to Appalachia Parking. The Valley Way is the easiest and shortest option.

Second Option

Level of difficulty:	⌂⌂
Total distance:	*24.2 km*
Time:	*3 days*
Change in altitude:	*1,060 m*
Starting point:	*Crawford Depot at Appalachia Parking.*

Day One: (14.5 km) from the Crawford Depot parking lot to Hermit Lake, via Crawford Path, Tuckerman Crossover and Tuckerman Ravine Trail.

Day Two: (13 km) from Hermit Lake to Crag Camp via Tuckerman Ravine, Gulfside and Spur trails.

Day Three: (5.3 km) from Crag Camp to the Appalachia Parking via Spur Trail, Randolph Path and Air Line.

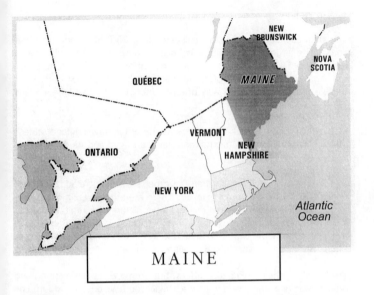

MAINE

The state of Maine has a very distinctive geography. Several mountain ranges rise up amidst its numerous forests, where over 6,000 lakes and ponds make for a vacationer's paradise. The northern part of the state boasts the loveliest of these forests, as well as the highest mountain, Mount Katahdin (1,605 m), and the largest lake, Moosehead (64 km long). Maine is most famous, however, for its magnificent coast, with its hundreds of islands and little peninsulas, not to mention all the beaches in the southern part of the state. This wonderful coast stretches 360 km, but you'd have to cover over 5,500 km to explore all its little nooks and crannies.

The celebrated Acadia National Park lies here, along this shore lapped by the Atlantic Ocean. This park, located on Mount Desert Island, offers breathtaking scenery, numerous historical attractions and an extensive network of hiking trails, enabling visitors to explore the most beautiful mountaintops on the island.

Like the other New England states, Maine is sparsely populated (pop. 1,200,000) and has pleasant little villages where time seems to have little hold on the daily life of local inhabitants. One obvious exception is the super-touristy southern beach region (Old Orchard, Wells, Ogunquit, York, etc.), which attract droves of sun-worshipping vacationers.

The state capital is Augusta, a small city (pop. 20,000) inland from the coast. The largest city in Maine is Portland (pop. 64,000), which was founded in 1632 and destroyed on three different occasions, once by the Amerindians (1676), once by the English (1775) and once by a terrible fire (1866). Maine was officially recognized as an independent state in 1820.

Not as busy or as popular with hikers as the other New England states, Maine still has a lot to offer. Its mountains are wild and its countryside is diverse.

Maine is a bit farther afield than the other states, but avid hikers will find it well worth the extra mileage. There are at least six hiking areas in the state. We have included the two most picturesque regions. Baxter Park, in northern Maine, is home to the famous Mount Katahdin, the highest peak in the state. Acadia National Park, located in Southern Maine on Mount Desert Island, is also described.

The terrain of these two parks differs, but both are equally exciting and representative of the diversity of the Maine countryside. The mountains of Baxter Park are rather imposing and the altitude changes are significant. As such the most interesting hikes here are also the most difficult ones and only experienced hikers should attempt them.

Baxter Park

Baxter Park is a state park and therefore maintained by the government of Maine. It is quite isolated and there are no major towns within close proximity. The closest town is Millinocket (29 km away) and the nearest city is Bangor (144 km from the park).

Baxter Park exists due to the generosity of Governor Percival P. Baxter, who donated the land to the state in 1931. In return he requested that it remain undeveloped and that the area be designated a wildlife sanctuary. He also requested that the park be visited only by lovers of nature and of the outdoors. It is out of respect for this ecological vision that the area surrounding the park remains sparsely developed and that the 80 km of roads through the park remain unpaved.

Today Baxter Park covers more than 81,000 ha. It is about 32 km wide and 48 km long. Throughout the park there are 46 summits of more than 1000 m, and 288 km of marked and maintained trails.

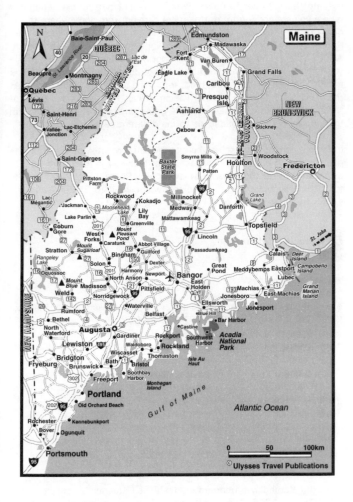

Finding Your Way Around

It is not easy to get to Baxter Park. There are two routes depending where you are coming from. If you are coming from somewhere to the north of the park take Route 27 then Route 16 to North Anson, then Route 201A North to Bingham. At Bingham take Route 16 East to Abbot Village and then Route 6-15 North to Greenville. At Greenville you have to follow a small road to Kokadjo. Just after the town there is a gate: this is a private forest road, for which there is an $8 US toll. At the next gate follow the road linking Baxter Park with the town of Millinocket. Follow the signs for the gate house at Togue Point. From this entrance a small road leads to the different campgrounds.

If you are coming from somewhere to the south or west of the park, the route is much easier. The closest major highway is Interstate 95. On Interstate 95, at the town of Medway take Route 11-157 East to the town of Millinocket. From there follow the road to Baxter Park, and watch for signs for the gate house at Togue Pond.

 Practical Information

■ **Useful Addresses**

● Baxter State Park: Reservation Clerk, 64 Balsam Drive, Millinocket, Maine 04462, (☎ *207-723-5140*).

● Maine Appalachian Trail Club, P.O. Box 283, Augusta, Maine 04330.

 Exploring

■ **Greenville**

Visit the Moosehead Marine Museum ☎ (207) 695-2716.

Visit the **Katahdin**, a restored old-fashioned steamship, built in 1914 ☎ (207) 695-2716. The ship is used for cruises on the lake.

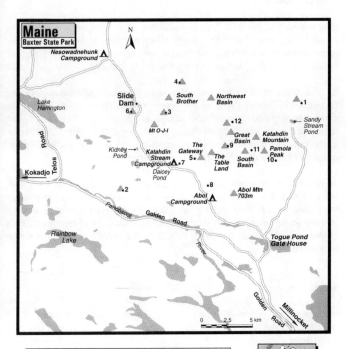

1. South Turner Mountain
2. Sentinel Mountain
3. Mount Coe
4. North Brother Mountain
5. Owl Mountain
6. Doubletop Mountain
7. Hunt Trail
8. Abol Trail
9. Baxter Peak
10. Knife Edge
11. Chimney Pond Trail
    Dudley Trail
    Cathedral Trail
    Saddle Trail
12. Hamlin Peak

Accommodations

■ Reservations

Space is limited, particularly in the shelters. Reservations, often months in advance, are therefore strongly recommended. Reservations by telephone are not accepted, since you have to write to the park service for documentation, and advance payment is required.

It is a good idea to be well-informed of park regulations. Pets are forbidden in Baxter Park, as are power boats, motor bikes and other small motorized vehicles. Trailer access is also limited. Canoes may be rented at South Branch Pond, Russell Pond, and Daicey Pond. Admission to the park is $8 to $10 per car. There is also a fee for the use of camp-grounds, cabins and shelters *($4 to $25 per person)*.

The park is open year-round. During the winter it is a popular spot with mountain-climbers. The rules for the distribution of climbing permits are very strict. Each hiker must send proof of climbing experience several months in advance. These regulations exist because of numerous fatal climbing accidents in the past, as well as the recent increase of traffic in the area.

■ Camping

In Baxter Park, you may camp in a tent, lean-to, shelter, or lodge. Each of these options can be found at the campsites. There are nine campsites throughout the park, accommodating a total of more than 700 people. Seven of the sites are accessible by car, the other two are accessible only by foot. All of the sites are very basic: no hot water, no supply stores, no gas and no treated water.

By Car

- Roaring Brook
- Abol
- Katahdin Stream
- Nesowadnehunk
- South Branch Pond
- Daicey Pond
- Trout Brook Farm

By Foot

- Russell Pond
- Chimney Pond

■ **Private Camping**

Greenville

Lily Bay State Park (☎ *207-824-2836)*: small state campground, with no showers, and quite far from Baxter Park.

Millinocket-Medway

Katahdin Shadows Campground (☎ *207-746-9349)*
Pine Grove Campground (☎ *207-746-5172)*

■ **Hotels, Motels, Inns ...**

Millinocket

Heritage Motor Inn (☎ *207-723-9777)*
The Atrium Inn (☎ *207-723-4555)*
Pamola Motor Lodge (☎ *207-723-9746)*

 Short Hikes

Most of the hikes in Baxter Park are difficult. Baxter Park is not the place to introduce a beginner to the joys of hiking, and the time it takes to reach the park is prohibitive for casual outings.

The focal point of any visit to Baxter Park is of course Mount Katahdin and its surroundings. The hikes we have chosen are in this area, as well as on the adjacent peaks. These less difficult hikes offer some of the most spectacular views of Katahdin and the entire region. These hikes can all be done in one day - just pack a lunch, a camera, and some extra clothing.

Before choosing a hike, make sure the appropriate accommodations are available. Access to some of the longer hikes is forbidden after 9am.

■ **South Turner Mountain**

Level of difficulty:	⌃⌃
Total distance:	*6.4 km*
Time:	*3 hours*
Change in altitude:	*500 m*
Starting point:	*Roaring Brook Camping, on the east side of Mount Katahdin, 13 km north of the Togue Pond gate house. Access to certain trails forbidden after 9am.*

South Turner Mountain (952 m) is located northeast of Mount Katahdin. Many hikers choose to climb this mountain on their first day out since it is easy to get to and offers spectacular views of Katahdin.

The path is called South Turner Trail, howeverthough from Roaring Brook Campground it follows Russell Pond Trail for 300 m. Then the trail climbs steadily up to Sandy Stream Pond, a favourite moose haunt. After 1.1 km, there is an intersection, beyond which cairns and markers indicate the way. At 2.4 km, the trail passes close to a spring. Shortly thereafter the trail emerges from the bush and curves up to the summit (3.2 km). From here the views of Mount Katahdin and the bowl are spectacular. Return by the same trail.

■ **Sentinel Mountain**

Level of difficulty:	⌃
Total distance:	*9.6 km*
Time:	*4 hours*
Change in altitude:	*250 m*
Starting point:	*Daicey Pond (or from Kidney Pond, for a shorter hike).*

Sentinel Mountain is situated west of Mount Katahdin. The hike up this small mountain is easy and offers a great view of the more picturesque, western slope of Mount Katahdin. The road leading from Daicey Pond to the main trail, Sentinel Landing, is not very well maintained. The trail begins 1.1 km along the road, and is fairly flat. It travels over a beaver-dammed river that must be crossed via stepping stones. The trail then rises gradually up to a curve not far from the summit (4.8 km). Near the summit there is a small, loop trail along which are some beautiful look out points. Return by the same trail.

■ Mount Coe

Level of difficulty:	⌃⌃
Total distance:	*10.6 km*
Time:	*6 hours*
Change in altitude:	*775 m*
Starting point:	*Slide Dam, near the picnic shelters, on the park road, 9,4 km north of Katahdin Stream Camping.*

Mount Coe is northwest of Mount Katahdin, just north of Mount O-J-I. The hike up is quite difficult but once at the summit a spectacular view makes it all worthwhile. To begin, follow the densely wooded Marston Trail uphill to an intersection (1.9 km). Turn right onto Mount Coe Trail. In 1932, following a rough storm, a landslide swept across this section of the trail, transforming it into the steep, rough terrain it is today. There is a second intersection (4.5 km), with a path leading to the summit of Mount O-J-I, the trail continues to the summit of Mount Coe (5.3 km). Return by the same trail.

Variations: This hike may be done as a loop by heading down the north side of Mount Coe and returning by Marston Trail. This adds 1.1 km.

At the second intersection, take a small detour to the summit of Mount O-J-I and back again to the intersection. This adds 2.2 km.

■ North Brother Mountain

Level of difficulty:	⌃⌃
Total distance:	*12 km*
Time:	*6 hours*
Change in altitude:	*890 m*
Starting point:	*Slide Dam, near the picnic shelters, on the park road, 9.4 km north of Katahdin Stream Camping.*

North Brother Mountain's crest is bare and provides a spectacular 360 ° view. This mountain, northwest of Katahdin, will thrill hikers looking for more adventurous climbing. It is not uncommon for its summit to be covered with a blanket of snow, even at the beginning of June!

The route follows Marston Trail, rising gradually to a first intersection (1.9 km), with the trail leading to Mount Coe. Further along it passes by a pond (3.2 km). From here the trail steepens with a few beautiful views along the way. Past another intersection (4.6 km) the trail flattens out, then steepens again up to some large boulders before reaching the summit (6 km). From this vantage point the view of Mount Katahdin, and everything else on the horizon, is superb. Return by the same trail.

Variation: On the way down from the summit of North Brother it is possible to take a detour up to the top of South Brother. This adds 1.6 km.

■ Owl Mountain

Level of difficulty:	
Total distance:	*10.6 km*
Time:	*4 h 30 min*
Change in altitude:	*780 m*
Starting point:	*Katahdin Stream Camping, 12.3 km north-west of the Togue Pond gate house.*

Owl Mountain is the first hill west of Mount Katahdin. It is relatively easy to get to and offers a spectacular panoramic view.

Start off on Hunt Trail, part of the Appalachian Trail, which ascends the southwest side of Mount Katahdin. The trail is fairly level to the first intersection (1.8 km), where you turn left. The trail eventually passes alongside a small stream (2.6 km) where you can replenish your water bottle. This is the last water source on the trail. The path then heads up a rather precipitous slope until it finally opens up to the first of the summit vistas (5 km). A few rises beyond is the peak of Owl Mountain (5.3 km). Return by the same trail.

■ Doubletop Mountain

Level of difficulty:	
Total distance:	*10.6 km*
Time:	*5 hours*
Change in altitude:	*720 m*
Starting point:	*Nesowadnehunk Campground, 26.8 km northwest of the Togue Pond gate house.*

Doubletop Mountain has, as its name suggests, two peaks, one to the south and one to the north, with only 300 m between. The climb on the north side of the mountain is the shorter one, while the south-side trail is difficult to follow in certain areas. From the top of the mountain the view, particularly of the summits to the east (O-J-I, Coe, and the Brothers) is exceptional.

The first 1.6 km of the trail are relatively flat. There is a gradual ascent through the valley that separates Doubletop from Veto Mountain to the west. The trail follows the northern ridge of Doubletop Mountain, becoming increasingly precipitous until it reaches the northern summit (5 km). It continues for a short distance to the southern peak (5.3 km). Return by the same trail.

Variation: It is possible to hike over Doubletop Mountain by going up one side and coming down the other, either north to south or vice versa. You will, however, need two cars: one parked at Foster Field near the bridge crossing the Nesowadnehunk River and the other at Nesowadnehunk Campground. It is 11.3 km from one side to the other, a hike of six to seven hours.

■ **Mount Katahdin**

In Abenaki, the aboriginal language of the area, Katahdin means "the biggest mountain", and Mount Katahdin is indeed the highest peak in Maine. The first known climb of the mountain was accomplished in 1804, by a group of eleven hikers.

While Mount Katahdin's 1,605 m do not quite measure up to Mount Washington's 1,906 m, its northern location gives it similar harsh weather conditions. As well, most trails leading to the summit are very difficult with considerable altitude changes (up to 1,220 m!).

Seasoned hikers confirm that Mount Katahdin is the most fascinating mountain in New England. Its isolated location, weather conditions, steep, rough trails, and magnificent views make it virtually sacred ground to avid hikers and nature lovers alike.

Mount Katahdin has something few mountains can claim: this one mountain is comprised of six peaks. The highest, Baxter Peak (1,605 m), is on the western side of the mountain. Right beside it, to the south, is South Peak (1,597 m). To the east are Chimney Peak and

Pamola Peak (1,494 m). To the north are Hamlin Peak (1,448 m) and the Howe Peaks (1,443 m and 1,406 m).

There is a 1.8 km-long ridge connecting the two highest peaks, Baxter Peak and Pamola Peak. The ridge is called Knife Edge, and with good reason since it is less than one metre wide in some spots and can be very dangerous in bad weather. Knife Edge is considered the most spectacular trail in all of New England.

Mount Katahdin is one terminus of the Appalachian Trail which links it to Mount Springer, 3,260 km away, in Georgia!

There are more than ten trails covering the various peaks of Mount Katahdin. The trails suggested below all leave from one of the four campgrounds at the foot of Mount Katahdin, specifically, Katahdin Stream Campground, Abol Campground, Roaring Brook Campground, and Chimney Pond Campground.

Hunt Trail

Level of difficulty:	🔺🔺🔺
Total distance:	*16.8 km*
Time:	*8 h 30 min*
Change in altitude:	*1,245 m*
Starting point:	*Katahdin Stream Campground.*

Katahdin Stream Campground is located on the west side of Mount Katahdin, 12.3 km northwest of the park entrance at Togue Pond. The route to the summit of Baxter Peak is called Hunt Trail and makes up a section of the Appalachian Trail. The 8.4 km from Katahdin Stream Campground to Baxter Peak is quite difficult.

Hunt Trail was cleared in 1900 by Irving O. Hunt who was working in a camp near the Sourdnahunk River. It rises gradually to the first intersection (1.8 km) then steepens to a small cave formed by two large boulders. The trail continues on rock bed, marked by cairns, through large boulders to a place called the Gateway (6 km).

At Thoreau Spring (6.7 km) you can refill your water bottle, provided the season is not too dry. Near the spring is the last intersection, from which Baxter Peak Cutoff skirts the summit.

Hunt Trail climbs slowly and leads directly to the summit of Baxter Peak (8.4 km), where the view is truly spectacular. Return by the same trail.

Abol Trail

Level of difficulty:	🏔🏔🏔
Total distance:	*14.5 km*
Time:	*9 hours*
Change in altitude:	*1,216 m*
Starting point:	*Abol Campground.*

Abol Campground is located on the southwest side of Mount Katahdin, 9 km northwest of the Gate House at Togue Pond. The only trail leaving from Abol Campground is the Abol Trail, which leads to Baxter Peak, Mount Katahdin's highest.

It is 6 km from Abol Campground to Baxter Peak. Abol Trail joins Hunt Trail (after 4.5 km) and follows it to the summit.

Abol Trail is considered the oldest of the trails leading to the top of Mount Katahdin. This trail is very difficult and can be dangerous because of frequent rock slides. It is therefore recommended to head up by way of Abol Trail and to descend by Hunt Trail and the road. By walking a loop the treacherous Abol Trail descent is avoided. The loop is 14.5 km long and will take about 9 hours. It is one of the most difficult hikes.

Baxter Peak

Level of difficulty:	🏔🏔🏔
Total distance:	*13.8 km*
Time:	*8 h 30 min*
Change in altitude:	*1,147 m*
Starting point:	*Roaring Brook Campground.*

Roaring Brook Campground is located on the east side of Mount Katahdin, 13 km north of the Gate House at Togue Pond. Several trails start at this site. We have listed only the three most important and widely used ones. The first leads to the summit of Baxter Peak, the highest on Mount Katahdin and in the whole State. It is a very difficult trail and follows the spectacular Knife Edge Ridge for part of its length.

From roaring Brook Campground follow Chimney Pond Trail, Taylor Trail, and Knife Edge Trail. It is 13.8 km return and very difficult.

Follow Chimney Pond Trail for 160 m. Then take Taylor Trail which quickly becomes very steep and unprotected. It crosses a small stream and then rises steadily. The trail follows the rocky ridge up to the summit of Pamola Peak (5 km), from which the view, especially of narrow Knife Edge Ridge, is spectacular.

Caution: Hikers are discouraged from following Taylor Trail in bad weather because it is too exposed. Most of the trail is rock and therefore slippery when wet, especially on the way down.

Knife Edge

Level of difficulty:	
Total distance:	*1.8 km*
Time:	*2 h*
Change in altitude:	*110 m*
Starting point:	*Pamola Peak.*

From Pamola Peak take Knife Edge Trail to Baxter Peak. This trail is only 1.8 km long but on a clear day provides one of the most spectacular hikes in the eastern United States. This narrow ridge, only one metre wide in some spots and bordered by a cliff, links Pamola Peak and Baxter Peak, by way of Chimney Peak and South Peak.

From Pamola Peak follow the cairns southwest. The trail descends into a rocky fissure and then climbs towards Chimney Peak. It then leads directly to South Peak, and then Baxter Peak (6,9 km). Return by the same trail.

Caution: Knife Edge Trail can be dangerous in bad weather, particularly in high winds.

Variation: If the weather is threatening or you would simply prefer a looped trail, it is possible to descend the northeastern side of the mountain from Baxter Peak. This involves following Saddle Trail and Chimney Pond Trail. This hike is longer, 15.8 km in total, but much easier so the time required is the same.

Chimney Pond Trail

Level of difficulty:	⌃
Total distance:	*5.3 km*
Time:	*2 hours*
Change in altitude:	*430 m*
Starting point:	*Roaring Brook Campground.*

The second trail leads to Chimney Pond Campground, an ideal, but often full, stop-over point for many hikes.

It is 5.3 km from Roaring Brook campground to Chimney Pond Campground via Chimney Pond Trail. This is an easy trail and takes 1 h 30 min.

Chimney Pond Trail is used mainly by hikers heading to Chimney Pond Campground. It is also used by hikers on their way to Hamlin Peak.

The trail rises gradually and presents few difficulties. There are two intersections along the way (at 3.7 km and at 4.8 km); keep left at both of them.

Hamlin Peak

Level of difficulty:	⌃ ⌃ ⌃
Total distance:	*14.4 km*
Time:	*7 hours*
Change in altitude:	*990 m*
Starting point:	*Roaring Brook Campground.*

The third trail leads to the summit of Hamlin Peak (1,448 m). There are many trails to the summit of Hamlin Peak, the busiest one, mentioned above, starts from Chimney Pond Campground. The one recommended here leaves from Roaring Brook Campground and follows Hamlin Ridge Trail, scaling the east side of Hamlin Peak.

To begin the hike, follow Chimney Pond Trail for 3.7 km or up to the first intersection. Take the right hand trail called North Basin Cutoff. After passing the beaver dams the trail comes to another intersection. This time go left to Hamlin Ridge Trail. This path follows the ridge to Hamlin Peak (7.2 km) and some great views. Return by the same trail.

Dudley Trail

Level of difficulty:	⋀⋀⋀
Total distance:	*3.9 km*
Time:	*4 hours*
Change in altitude:	*727 m*
Starting point:	*Chimney Pond Campground.*

Chimney Pond Campground is located at an altitude of 890 m, on Mount Katahdin itself. From here, the trails leading to the various summits of Mount Katahdin are often much shorter than those elsewhere in the park. There is, however, no road leading to the campground so any baggage must be carried into the area. The easiest trail to Chimney Pond Campground is Chimney Pond Trail which leaves from Roaring Brook Campground. It is 5.3 km to Chimney Pond Campground.

This campground is very popular. If you plan on staying here you will have to reserve very early. Campfires and tents are prohibited. You will have to stay in one of the lean-tos or the shelter, and you will need a campstove.

There are three trails from Chimney Pond Campground to the main summit of Katahdin, Baxter Peak; they are Dudley trail, Cathedral Trail and Saddle Trail. The first two are very difficult, the other is easier. Choose a trail according to the weather and your physical condition. A loop is also possible, by using the easy trail for the descent.

Dudley Trail is the most spectacular and the most difficult. From Chimney Pond Campground follow it to Pamola Peak (2 km). From there follow Knife Edge Trail to Baxter Peak (3.8 km). This trip will take three to four hours. Once at the summit you have three options for the trip back down to Chimney Pond Campground:

- Return by the same trail (about three hours).
- Descend by Cathedral Trail (not recommended as a way down).
- Descend by Saddle Trail, the quickest and easiest option, and the only choice in bad weather. The trail is 3.5 km and takes less than an hour and a half.

Cathedral Trail

Level of difficulty:	⌃⌃
Total distance:	*2.6 km*
Time:	*2 h 30 min*
Change in altitude:	*727 m*
Starting point:	*Chimney Pond Campground.*

The second option from Chimney Pond Campground is Cathedral Trail, and it is as spectacular as the first. It leads to three rocky points, known as the Cathedral Rocks, which offer commanding views of the famous Knife Edge. It is 2.6 km from the campground to Baxter Peak, following Saddle Trail near the end. Expect about two and a half hours for the hike up.

The return to Chimney Pond Campground can be made by the same trail (not recommended), by Knife Edge and Dudley Trail, visually stunning but very difficult, or by Saddle Trail, the quickest and easiest route.

Saddle Trail

Level of difficulty:	⌃
Total distance:	*3.5 km*
Time:	*2 hours*
Change in altitude:	*727 m*
Starting point:	*Chimney Pond Campground.*

The third and easiest trail from Chimney Pond Campground to Baxter Peak is Saddle Trail. Less impressive than the other two, it still has plenty to offer. The hike up is quick (2 hours), and Saddle Trail is the best choice for the descent. It is therefore usually included in a loop.

Acadia National Park

Acadia National Park is located in southeastern Maine on the Atlantic coast. It is one of the best places to incorporate hiking into a family vacation as there are a variety of interesting and easy hikes.

Since it is a national park, Acadia is very well organized and offers a whole slew of activities for the whole family. The park is located on Mount Desert Island, which is linked to the mainland by a bridge. The island is 25.6 km long and 20.8 km wide, with a total area of 14,170 ha.

Mount Desert Island is shaped like a bear's paw and is divided into two sections (east and west) by an inlet called Somes Sound (the only fjord on the American east coast). There are 17 mountains and more than 160 km of maintained and marked trails for hiking.

The mountains range in height from 120 m to 450 m, but since the park is so close to the sea you do not have to climb very high to enjoy spectacular views. Most of the trails are accessible to beginners and can be walked in a half-day. The only difficult and potentially dangerous trail is Precipice Trail on Mount Champlain. The trails are all classified by the Appalachian Mountain Club (AMC).

There are also some interesting cliff walks along the seashore. These walks are pleasant and refreshing, and offer views that are certain to impress. Find out the tide schedule to avoid any unpleasant surprises!

There are two beaches on the island, one at Echo Lake on the western side of the island, and Sand Beach on the eastern side. The sand here is very fine, but the water is quite cold.

Samuel de Champlain, the founder of Québec, named the island Mount Desert in 1604. The Abenaki Indians called it Pemetic Island which means "sloping land".

Acadia National Park exists today thanks to the efforts of George B. Dorr, also known as the "father of Acadia National Park". From 1901 until his death, in 1944, he worked tirelessly to establish and enlarge the boundaries of the park. In 1916 the Sieur de Monts National Monument was created. In 1919 the island became a national park, the first east of the Mississippi, and, in 1929, it was finally named Acadia National Park.

In 1917, John D. Rockefeller Jr. had an 80 km unpaved road constructed for the sole use of nature-lovers. The road, called Carriage Path, is closed to cars, providing a peaceful route for hikers, cyclists and skiers. There are sixteen stone bridges along the road, which blend harmoniously with the natural environment.

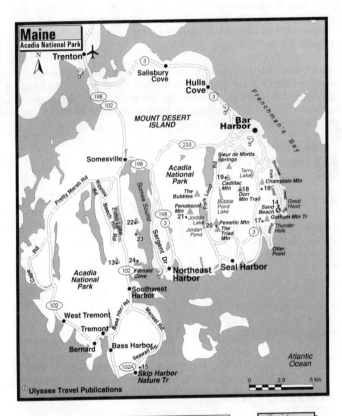

Finding Your Way Around

When coming from the north, many choose to drive through the White Mountains (in New Hampshire and home of Mount Washington) to cut the drive in two. As well as spending the night here you may want to do a few hikes in the area.

The closest major highway to Acadia National Park is Interstate 95, which is accessible via Route 201 from the north or Route 302 from the west. Once on Interstate 95 head east to Bangor. From Bangor take the 395 then 1A South to Ellsworth, then Route 3 South to the Mount Desert Island bridge, Acadia National Park. See map p 175.

 Practical Information

■ **Camping Store**

Cadillac Mountain Sports
26 Cottage Street
Bar Harbor
☎ (207) 288-4532

■ **Tourist Information**

Acadia National Park
P. O. Box 177
Bar Harbor, Maine 04609
☎ (207) 288-3338

Acadia National Park Rangers
☎ (207) 288-3360

On site

Acadia National Park Visitor Center, on Route ME 3 at Hulls Cove near Bar Harbor.

Thompson Island Information Center, located at the entrance to the park, on Route 3.

 Exploring

Drive along beautiful Park Loop Road.

Visit the **Abbe Museum** (☎ *207-288-3519*) of native culture.

Take a whale watching cruise, or sunset cruise (☎ *1-800-421-3307 or 207-288-9776*).

Visit the **Mount Desert Oceanarium** (☎ *207-288-5005*).

Visit the museum of natural history located at the **College of the Atlantic** (☎ *207-288-5015*).

Visit the town of Bar Harbor with its interesting boutiques, restaurants, bars, and theatres, and its quaint side streets leading to the sea.

Mountain bikes may be rented in Bar Harbor, or you can take a cruise in the harbour.

 Accommodations

■ **Camping**

There are two public campsites in Acadia National Park. The first is the **Blackwoods Campground**, located in the southeast corner of the eastern side of the island. The second is the **Seawall Campground** (☎ *1-900-370-5566*), located in the southern end of the west side of the island. These sites are almost always full so you may have to opt for one of the eleven private campgrounds on the island. This list is also available at the park entrance.

■ **Private Camping**

Mount Desert Camping *(☎ 207-244-3710)*: best location
Narrows Too Camping Resort *(☎ 207-667-4300)*
Barcadia Tent & Trailer Grounds *(☎ 207-288-3520)*
Mount Desert Narrows Camping Resort *(☎ 207-288-4782)*
Hadley's Point Camping *(☎ 207-288-4808)*
Spruce Valley Camping *(☎ 207-288-5139)*
Bar Harbor Camping *(☎ 207-288-5185)*
Somes Sound View Camping *(☎ 207-244-3890)*
Smuggler's Den *(☎ 207-244-3944)*
The White Birches Camping *(☎ 207-244-3797)*
Bass Harbor Camping *(☎ 207-244-5875)*

■ **Hotels, Motels, Inns ...**

Bar Harbor

Castlemaine Inn *(☎ 207-288-4563)*: located in downtown Bar Harbor, bed and breakfast in historic building (1886).

Cadillac Motor Inn *(☎ 207-288-3831)*: motel rooms at a reasonable price.

Cromwell Harbor Motel *(☎ 207-288-3201)*: quiet pleasant atmosphere.

The Hearthside Bed & Breakfast *(☎ 207-288-4533)*: located in downtown Bar Harbor, in a turn-of-the-century home.

 Short Hikes

The hikes suggested are mostly short and easy. Since they are all relatively short and safe there is little or no accompanying description.

■ **Beech Mountain**

Beech Mountain Trail

Level of difficulty:	
Total distance:	*2.9 km*
Time:	*1 h 5 min*
Change in altitude:	*100 m*
Starting point:	*Beech Cliff parking lot, west of Echo Lake.*

This is a short loop with some beautiful views. Take the north fork up and the south fork (which is shorter) down.

■ **Great Head Trail**

Level of difficulty:	
Total distance:	*2 km*
Time:	*45 min*
Change in altitude:	*40 m*
Starting point:	*Sand Beach parking lot.*

This short hike follows the oceanside cliffs east of Sand Beach to Great Head, a small promontory at the end of the peninsula.

The trail then rises northward to an intersection. Turn left to return to Sand Beach.

■ **Ocean Trail**

Level of difficulty:	
Total distance:	*5.8 km*
Time:	*2 h*
Change in altitude:	*nil*
Starting point:	*Sand Beach parking lot.*

This trail starts at the western end of Sand Beach near the stairs. It follows the shore (on the cliff top), about 3 km, to Otter Point. Along the way it passes Thunder Hole, where the waves come crashing into an inlet in the cliff.

At the end of the trail it is possible to return either by backtracking or by following Park Loop Drive.

■ **Ship Harbor**

Level of difficulty:	⛰
Total distance:	*1.5 km*
Time:	*45 min*
Change in altitude:	*nil*
Starting point:	*Ship Harbor Nature Trail parking lot on Route 102A, south of Southwest Harbor.*

This is a quaint little trail which winds along the coast to an area where the ocean pours inland sculpting small inlets and tidal pools.

■ **Mount Champlain**

Precipice Trail

Level of difficulty:	⛰⛰⛰
Total distance:	*1.3 km*
Time:	*1 h 15 min*
Change in altitude:	*300 m*
Starting point:	*at the foot of Mount Champlain (east side) on Park Loop Road.*

Mount Champlain (322 m) is located south of Bar Harbor, near the sea. Precipice Trail, the most difficult trail in the park, climbs the mountain's steep eastern slope. There are many trails leading to the summit of Mount Champlain from both the north and south sides.

This trail is very steep. It climbs directly up the eastern slope to the summit. The first part, to the intersection at 640 m, is relatively easy. At the intersection turn left and use the ladders attached to the rock faces to assist you. The trail here is more like a rock climb than a hike, and the requisite caution should be applied.

If you suffer from vertigo, avoid this trail! Also, shorter people may have trouble reaching the handholds.

From the summit it is possible to descend by Bear Brook Trail to the north, taking Precipice Trail again at the intersection.

Beachcroft Trail

Level of difficulty:	⛰
Total distance:	*2.6 km*
Time:	*1 h 45 min*
Change in altitude:	*300 m*
Starting point:	*on Route 3, at the parking lot just north of the small lake called The Tarn.*

This trail climbs the northwestern slope of Mount Champlain and offers a wide open view almost all the way up. The trail passes under the summit of Huguenot Head (220 m) and climbs again to the top of Mount Champlain. Return by the same trail.

Beehive Trail

Level of difficulty:	⛰ ⛰
Total distance:	*1.9 km*
Time:	*45 min*
Change in altitude:	*150 m*
Starting point:	*in front of the Sand Beach parking lot.*

This trail leads up to a beautiful lookout with Sand Beach at its feet and Frenchman's Bay stretching out before it. The trail is short but also quite difficult, and ladders are needed. For the return continue northwest to an intersection. Go left to descend to Park Loop Road.

■ Gorham Mountain

Level of difficulty:	⛰
Total distance:	*3.2 km*
Time:	*1 h 15 min*
Change in altitude:	*150 m*
Starting point:	*Gorham Mountain parking lot on Park Loop Road.*

Gorham Mountain Trail climbs gradually to an intersection at 480 m. The trail to the right, called Cadillac Cliffs, makes a short loop and returns to Gorham Mountain Trail. The summit is a bit further north (1.6 km). It is bare and offers a spectacular view. Return by the same trail.

Variation: It is possible to go from the top of Gorham Mountain to the summit of Mount Champlain by following Bear Brook Trail. It is 2.4 km one way and takes about an hour.

■ **Dorr Mountain**

Level of difficulty:	
Total distance:	*4.8 km*
Time:	*2 h 15 min*
Change in altitude:	*363 m*
Starting point:	*Sieur de Monts Spring.*

The trail crosses two intersections, the first at 800 m, the second at 1.8 km. It then becomes more exposed and steepens to the summit of Dorr Mountain (2.4 km). Return by the same trail.

Variation: The summit of Cadillac Mountain is accessible from the top of Dorr Mountain via Dorr Mountain Notch Trail. The trail is 1.4 km one way and takes about 45 minutes. From the Cadillac Mountain parking lot, this route is 7.6 km return, about 4 hours of hiking.

■ **Cadillac Mountain**

Cadillac Mountain South Ridge Trail

Level of difficulty:	
Total distance:	*11.2 km*
Time:	*4 h 30 min*
Change in altitude:	*424 m*
Starting point:	*on Route 3 just after the entrance to Blackwoods Campground.*

Cadillac Mountain is the tallest on the island (466 m), but it is also the busiest since there is a road giving cars access to the summit. The mountain is named after one of the island's celebrated personalities,

Antoine Laumet, who was titled Sieur Antoine de la Mothe Cadillac in 1688. He gained even greater fame in 1701, when he founded the city of Detroit. Of course the famous luxury automobile is also named after him.

The trail is long but not difficult. After 1.6 km there is a small loop at Eagle's Crag and a beautiful lookout. The trail meets another intersection at a spot called Featherbed (3.7 km) and then climbs straight to the summit of Cadillac Mountain (5.6 km). Return by the same trail.

Cadillac West Face Trail

Level of difficulty:	
Total distance:	*4.6 km*
Time:	*2 h 30 min*
Change in altitude:	*335 m*
Starting point:	*north of Bubble Pond Lake, Park Loop Road.*

This rather difficult trail is the shortest route, by foot, to the summit of Cadillac Mountain. The hike demands a sustained effort. The trail intersects (1.4 km) with Cadillac South Ridge Trail. Continue left, up to the summit of Cadillac Mountain (2.3 km). Return by the same trail.

■ **Pemetic Mountain**

Pemetic Mountain Trail

Level of difficulty:	
Total distance:	*6.4 km*
Time:	*2 h 30 min*
Change in altitude:	*292 m*
Starting point:	*on the Carriage Road between The Triad and Day Mountain.*

Pemetic Mountain (380 m) located south of Eagle Lake, offers some magnificent views. It is an easy hike, and the return is by the same trail.

Bubble-Pemetic Trail

Level of difficulty:	⛰
Total distance:	*1.6 km*
Time:	*1 hour*
Change in altitude:	*267 m*
Starting point:	*Bubble Rock parking lot, 1.8 km south of Bubble Pond.*

This trail rises gradually and joins Pemetic Mountain Trail after only 640 m. This point is just below the summit of Pemetic Mountain, a quick and easy 160 m away. Return by the same trail.

■ **Penobscot Mountain**

Jordan Cliffs Trail

Level of difficulty:	⛰⛰
Total distance:	*5.4 km*
Time:	*2 h 15 min*
Change in altitude:	*278 m*
Starting point:	*Jordan Pond House, south of Jordan Pond.*

Penobscot Mountain (364 m) has a bare summit that offers a spectacular view of the region.

This trail is quite difficult. It ascends the east side of the mountain, parallel to Penobscot Mountain Trail. Follow Penobscot Mountain Trail for the first 640 m, leaving it near Carriage Road. At the intersection just below the summit, turn left towards the top of Penobscot Mountain (2.7 km). From the intersection to the summit the trail is relatively difficult but offers a beautiful view of the area. Return by the same trail. It is also possible to descend by Penobscot Mountain Trail, which is easier and shorter.

Penobscot Mountain Trail

Level of difficulty:	⛰
Total distance:	*4.8 km*
Time:	*2 hour*

Change in altitude:	*278 m*
Starting point:	*Jordan Pond House.*

This trail, which also leads to the summit of Penobscot Mountain, is shorter and easier than Jordan Cliffs Trail. The last section of the trail is particularly striking since it skirts the rocky spur of the mountain. Return by the same trail.

Variation: The summit of Mount Sargent is accessible from the top of Penobscot via Sargent Pond Trail and the Sargent Mountain South Ridge Trail. This detour adds about 1.9 km, or 40 minutes, one-way.

■ **Acadia Mountain**

Acadia Mountain Trail

Level of difficulty:	
Total distance:	*3.2 km*
Time:	*1 h 15 min*
Change in altitude:	*176 m*
Starting point:	*Acadia Mountain Parking, on Route 102, 4.8 km south of Somesville.*

Acadia Mountain (208 m) is relatively small but nevertheless offers a spectacular view, particularly of Somes Sound.

Keep left at the intersection near the beginning of the trail (160 m). The trail climbs steadily and gradually opens up to the wonderful view at the summit. Return by the same trail.

Variation: Many hikers make a loop by continuing over the summit to Man O' War Brook Fire Road, arriving just a few steps from the parking lot on Route 102.

■ **Mount Saint Sauveur**

Ledge Trail

Level of difficulty:	
Total distance:	*2.6 km*
Time:	*1 h 10 min*

Change in altitude:	*145 m*
Starting point:	*St. Sauveur Parking, on Route 102, 320 m south of AMC Echo Lake Camp Road.*

This second small mountain (207 m) offers a great view for little effort.

The trail climbs slowly to an intersection (800 m) with St. Sauveur Trail, which leads to the summit (1.3 km) of St. Sauveur Mountain. The nicest lookout is just east of the summit at a spot called Eagle Cliff. Return by the same trail.

■ Flying Mountain

Flying Mountain Trail

Level of difficulty:	◩
Total distance:	*1 km*
Time:	*30 min*
Change in altitude:	*86 m*
Starting point:	*Fernald Cove parking lot.*

This is the smallest mountain in the area (87 m) but it has the most to offer. After just a few minutes walking there is a truly beautiful view. The small villages of Northeast and Southwest Harbor, Somes Sound, and a collection of tiny islands to the south spread out at your feet.

The trail climbs only slightly, and in 15 minutes you are at the summit. Return by the same trail.

Variation: It is possible to continue along the trail to Valley Cove and then return to the parking lot by way of Valley Cove Truck Road, making a loop of 1.9 km in total.

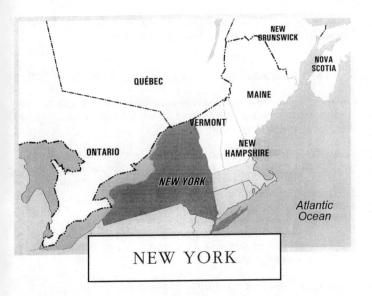

NEW YORK

With 18 million inhabitants, New York State has a population three times that of Quebec. If you leave New York City and its nearly 9 million residents out of the picture, however, the state no longer seems overpopulated. Its countryside and mountainous regions actually look much like those of Quebec and New England. These areas are scattered with pleasant little villages, whose residents are both friendly and helpful to visitors.

New York State is not one of the six states that make up New England (Vermont, New Hampshire, Maine, Massachusetts, Connecticut and Rhode Island). Stretching from Niagara Falls in the west to Lake Champlain in the east, it has an extremely varied landscape, and its inhabitants lead a wide range of lifestyles. The many nationalities found here make for an extremely rich culture, so that fascinating discoveries await visitors year-round.

The state capital is Albany, a city of 100,000 inhabitants located in the central part of the state, to the east, between New York City and Plattsburgh. The highest point in New York State is Mount Marcy (1,629 m), in the Adirondacks.

Don't forget that the speed limit on highways has recently been increased from 55 mi/h (85 km/h) to 65 mi/h (108 km/h).

The Adirondacks

Nicknamed the "Adis", Adirondack State Park covers 2,430,000 ha making it the largest park in the United States, excluding Alaska. It is as large as the state of Vermont!

This New York State park, 100 km south of the Canadian border, is not only a haven for hikers, but also attracts biking, canoeing, ornithology, rock-climbing, ice-climbing, cross-country skiing, and snowshoeing enthusiasts, as well as nature-lovers in general.

The park provides all of the necessary amenities for a vacation in the great outdoors. It is visited by hikers from the large cities of the northeastern United States — New York, Boston, Philadelphia and Buffalo — as well as many Canadians.

Adirondack State Park is divided into seven regions:

- High Peaks Region
- Northern Region
- Central Region
- Northville-Placid Region
- West-Central Region
- Eastern Region
- Southern Region

The hikes presented in this guide are all located in the High Peaks region. Situated in the northeastern section of the park, it is the region most popular with hikers since it includes the highest mountains in the park and in the state.

Some of these mountains have altitudes to be reckoned with. There are two summits higher than 1,500 m, Mount Marcy (1,629 m) and Algonquin Peak (1,559 m), as well as 46 summits higher than 1,200 m.

Even though these mountains are south of the Canadian border, their summits are nevertheless covered with alpine-arctic vegetation (mosses and lichens) common to more northern climes.

To explore these summits a huge network of trails has been developed which today includes some 634 km of marked hiking trails.

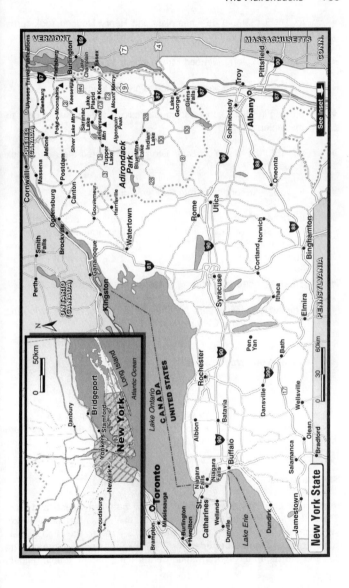

New York State

- In 1609, Samuel de Champlain and Henry Hudson took turns exploring the region.

- The first explorer climbed Mount Marcy in 1837.

- By 1850, the region was used mainly for logging.

- Starting in 1869, convalescing tuberculosis patients were sent to the region.

- In 1885, the New York State Legislature created the Adirondack Forest Preserve.

- In 1892, Adirondack State Park was created.

- In 1894, "Forever Wild" was incorporated into the constitution of the State of New York. It was the first time in the history of the United States that "Wild Land" was protected by a state constitution.

- The first Adirondack hiking guide was published in 1934.

- The Adirondack region, specifically Lake Placid, was twice the site of the Winter Olympics, in 1932 and 1980.

 Finding Your Way Around

The closest major highway to the Adirondacks is Interstate 87. From the 87 take Exit 34 at Keenesville and then 9N South to the town of Keene (164 km). The route from there depends on the hike you are doing.

■ **Parking lots**

Adirondak Loj: This parking lot is located between Keene and Lake Placid. From Keene take Route 73 towards Lake Placid for about 20 km and turn left (south) at the "Adirondak Loj, Trails to the High Peaks" sign. Follow Adirondak Loj Road for 7.7 km to the end. A large parking lot and the High Peaks Information Center (information, maps, guides,

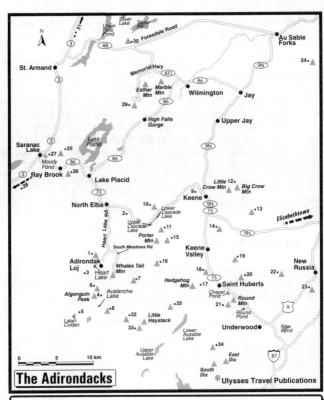

The Adirondacks

© Ulysses Travel Publications

1. Mount Jo
2. Mount Van Hoevenberg
3. Rocky Falls
4. Van Hoevenberg Trail
5. Avalanche Pass Trail
6. Wright Peak
7. Phelps Mountain
8. Mount Colden
9. Owl's Head Mountain
10. Pitchoff Mountain
11. Cascade Mountain
12. Crow Mountains
13. Hurricane Mountain
14. Baxter Mountain
15. Little Porter Mountain
16. Big Slide Mountain
17. Rooster Comb
18. Snow Mountain
19. Hopkins Mountain
20. Giant Mountain
21. Noonmark Mountain
22. Bald Peak
23. Gilligan Mountain
24. Poke-o-Moonshine
25. Mount Haystack
26. Scarface Mountain
27. Baker Mountain
28. Ampersand Mountain
29. Whiteface Mountain
30. Catamount Mountain
31. Silver Lake
32. Mount Marcy
33. Haystack Mountain
34. Dix Mountain
35. Gothics Mountain

food, showers, telephone, etc.) are located on the left. Cost of parking: $7 per day, $3.50 after 1pm.

The Adirondak Loj (inn, restaurant) is on the right, Heart Lake and camping are nearby.

Garden: This parking lot is located to the west of the town of Keene Valley, between the towns of Keene and Saint Huberts. From Keene take Route 73 to Keene Valley, located about 8 km to the south. In the centre of Keene Valley, turn right at the "Trail to the High Peaks" sign and drive along Interbrook Road for 2.6 km to the parking lot (keep right at the little bridge, about 1 km down the road).

Practical Information

■ Useful Addresses

Adirondack Trail Improvement Society (ATIS)
St. Huberts,
New York 12943

Department of Environmental Conservation (DEC)
Ray Brook,
New York 12977
☎ (518) 891-1370

New York State Police
☎ (518) 897-2000

New York State Forest Preserve Public Campgrounds DEC
50 Wolf Rd.,
Albany, New York 12233
A list of campgrounds in the region is available here.

■ Camping Stores

The Mountaineer
on Route 73 just before Keene Valley,
☎ (518) 576-2281

Eastern Mountain Sports
100 Main Street, Lake Placid,
☎ (518) 523-2505

■ **Hiking Club**

Adirondack Mountain Club (ADK): R.R. 3, P.O. Box 3055, Lake George, New York 12845-9532, ☎ (518) 668-4447, ✒ (518) 668-3746. Founded in 1922, the Adirondack Mountain Club has more than 10,000 members in several sub-groups. As well as hiking, the ADK informs its members on canoeing, rock-climbing and cross-country skiing. Six times a year the ADK publishes its magazine *Adirondac* which is available in specialty magazine stores.

 Exploring

Visit **High Falls Gorge** near Whiteface Mountain *(☎ 518-946-2278)*.

Take a boat tour of Lake Placid *(☎ 518-523-9704)*.

Visit the **Historic Museum of Lake Placid/North Elba** *(☎ 518-523-1608)*.

Visit the **Olympic Center** *(☎ 518-523-1655)*.

Visit the **Olympic Jumping Complex** and take an elevator ride up the 100 m tower *(☎ 518-523-1655)*.

Visit the **Adirondack Museum** at Blue Mountain Lake *(☎ 518-352-7311)*.

Drive to the summit of Whiteface Mountain by car, via the **Memorial Highway** *(☎ 518-946-7175)*.

 Accommodations

■ **Camping**

Sleeping in the Adirondacks is easy to do. You can camp under the stars, in a lean-to, or in a tent — and all for free! The only accommodation along the trails that has a fee is Johns Brook Lodge. A group of fewer than ten people does not need a permit to camp, sleep in a lean-to or build a fire. The designated areas for these activities must, however, be respected.

Groups of ten or more must obtain a permit to stay overnight. The park officials need to know that particular sites will be very busy on given dates. Rangers can then suggest alternative sites if those the group had planned to use are full. To obtain a permit write to the Department of Environmental Conservation, Ray Brook, New York 12977, USA. Count on a few weeks for processing and delivery of the permit.

Lake Placid

Adirondak Loj Campground (☎ 518-523-3441)
Whispering Pines Campground (☎ 518-523-9322)
Lake Placid-Whiteface Mt Koa (☎ 518-946-2171)

Wilmington

North Poles Campground (☎ 518-946-7733)
Twin Acres Campsites (☎ 518-946-7207)

Upper Jay

High Peaks Base Camp (☎ 518-946-2133)

■ Lodges

Johns Brook Lodge (JBL): The JBL is only accessible by foot. It is 5.6 km from Garden parking lot, located just to the west of the town of Keene Valley. It is open every day from mid-June to Labour Day (early-September), as well as on several weekends outside of this period. It is a good place to stop for a rest, to warm up, or to eat. To spend the night a reservation is recommended as this place is popular with hikers *($21 to $26 per night per person, breakfast included).*

Adirondak Loj : Adirondak Loj is located 14.4 km from Lake Placid and is accessible by car. In addition to the lodge there is the Camper's and

Hiker's Building, right next to the entrance to the parking lot, which houses a small store that sells hiking and camping equipment. Near Adirondak Loj is a private campsite with lean-tos. The lodge is open year-round and reservations are recommended *($25 to $30 per night per person, breakfast included)*.

Information and Reservations

Johns Brook Lodge (JBL) and **Adirondak Loj** *(P.O. Box 867, Lake Placid, New York 12946, ☎ 518-523-3441)*.

■ **Hotels, Motels, Inns ...**

Wilmington

Ledge Rock Motel facing Whiteface Mountain *(☎ 518-946-2302)*.
Grand View Motel *(☎ 518-946-2209)* with a beautiful view of Whiteface Mountain.

Lake Placid

Alpine Air Motel *(☎ 518-523-9261)*
Art Devlin's Olympic Motor Inn *(☎ 518-523-3700)*
Thunderbird Motor Inn *(☎ 518-523-2439)*
Mirror Lake Inn *(☎ 518-523-2544)* Luxury!

 Short Hikes

■ **Mount Jo**

Level of difficulty:	⛰
Total distance:	*3.7 km*
Time:	*1 h 30 min*
Change in altitude:	*212 m*
Starting point:	*from the parking lot of Adirondak Loj backtrack 100 m past the entrance and turn right at the Indian Pass Trail.*

Further along a sign indicates the direction for Mount Jo. Soon there is an intersection offering a choice between the Long Trail and the Short Trail. The Long Trail adds 450 m but is not as steep as the Short Trail and is therefore preferable for the ascent.

The trail climbs steadily and intersects again (1.6 km) with the Short Trail. Continue to the summit (1.8 km) for an exceptional view. The spectacular Cascade Mountains rise in the northeast, Mount Marcy in the southeast and Algonquin Peak in the southwest. Return by the same trail, or by the Short Trail to make a loop.

Located just north of Adirondak Loj, Mount Jo is a great place to introduce children to the joys of hiking. It is also a nice, short hike on which to use up extra energy at the end of the day. Its summit offers great views of the high peaks.

Mount Jo was named in 1877 by Henry Van Hoevenberg who christened it in honour of his fiance Josephine.

■ **Mount Van Hoevenberg**

Level of difficulty:	
Total distance:	*7 km*
Time:	*2 h 45 min*
Change in altitude:	*225 m*
Starting point:	*On South Meadow Road, 0.5 km from Adirondak Loj Road. South Meadow Road starts at Adirondak Loj Road, 6.1 km from Route 73 and 1.6 km from Adirondak Loj.*

Mount Van Hoevenberg rises up between two pretty stretches of grassland, North and South Meadows, visible on the left from Adirondak Loj Road. The mountain was named in anticipation of the 1932 Winter Olympics, after Henry Van Hoevenberg, who built the first Adirondack Lodge at the end of the previous century. It was on the north side of this mountain that the luge and bobsledding events were held.

The first part of the trail follows an old road and winds through the meadow, requiring little effort; the area can, however, be somewhat damp in the springtime. The trail then becomes a little more difficult and veers to the left and then to the right.

On its way to the summit, the path climbs up the western ridge of the mountain. Right before the top, you'll come to a lookout (3.4 km). You can see majestic Algonquin Peak (1,559 m), the second highest point in the Adirondacks, to the southeast, while Mount Marcy (1,628 m) dominates the horizon to the south. About 150 m farther, you'll reach the top of the mountain (872 m). Giant Mountain (1,410 m) and Porter Mountain (1,237 m) rise up to the east. Return by the same trail.

Variation: From the summit of Mount Van Hoevenberg, the trail heads down the north side of the mountain, offering hikers a look at both the old bobsled run and the newer one. The return trip adds a little over 5 km to the total distance of the hike, however. Keep in mind that you can also reach the bobsled run by car, via Route 73 (see Exploring, p 193).

■ **Rocky Falls**

Level of difficulty:	⛰
Total distance:	*7.7 km*
Time:	*2 h 30 min*
Change in altitude:	*nil*
Starting point:	*Adirondak Loj parking lot.*

Although not very high, the Rocky Falls are nonetheless very pleasant and refreshing on hot summer days. There is even a natural pool where you can go swimming. Don't be surprised, therefore to discover you're not the only one with the bright idea of soaking your sore feet here.

Starting at the Adirondak Loj parking lot, double back (100 m) past the entrance and turn right at the sign for Indian Pass Trail. Soon after, you'll come to an intersection where a path leads off to the top of Mount Jo. The main trail then runs along the north side of Heart Lake and crosses two cross-country ski trails.

Next, you'll enter a pretty forest, where the terrain is relatively flat. The trail crosses a stream and reaches an intersection. Take the trail to the right, which leads to Indian Pass, a lean-to and the Upper and Lower Rocky Falls, then heads back down to the main trail. Turn left to return to the first intersection, thus completing a small loop. Return by the same trail.

■ **Algonquin Peak**

Algonquin Peak (1,559 m) is the second highest summit in the Adirondacks, just shy of Mount Marcy's 1,629 m. Shaped like a pyramid, it is also one of the most magnificent mountains. The hikes up to the summit, from either side, are considered among the most beautiful in the northeast. On the bare mountaintop cairns mark the way to spectacular views of the whole region.

There are two routes to the summit of Algonquin Peak. Both take a day to complete and both leave from Adirondak Loj. The first route is 12.2 km and consists of a return trip along the same trail. The second is 18 km long. Both routes are considered very difficult. The second includes an arduous uphill section (720 m over 3.2 km).

Van Hoevenberg Trail

Level of difficulty:	⛰⛰⛰
Total distance:	*12.8 km*
Time:	*6 h 30 min*
Change in altitude:	*895 m*
Starting point:	*Adirondak Loj parking lot (see p 190).*

Follow Van Hoevenberg Trail to the first intersection (1.5 km) and then head towards Algonquin Peak. At 2.3 km the trail meets Whale's Tail Notch Ski Trail.

The trail crosses several small streams, then climbs steadily to a magnificent waterfall (to the left of the trail at 3.8 km). The trail continues uphill to an intersection (5 km), the left trail leading to Wright Peak. Beyond the intersection the real climbing begins. Past the timberline (5.7 km) the trail is indicated by cairns and yellow markers on rocks. In order to protect the fragile mountain vegetation it is important to stick to the trail. The trail continues around some large boulders to the summit (6.4 km). The view is staggering! Return by the same trail.

Avalanche Pass Trail

Level of difficulty:	⛰⛰⛰
Total distance:	*18.1 km*
Time:	*8 hours*

Change in altitude:	*895 m*
Starting point:	*Adirondak Loj parking lot (see p 190).*

This is a spectacular, but physically demanding, looped trail. Because of its sustained uphill climb this hike is not usually included in long trips requiring large backpacks.

Follow Van Hoevenberg Trail to Marcy Dam (3.7 km). On the southeast side of the dam, drinking water is available. Shortly after the dam is an intersection — follow Avalanche Pass Trail towards Lake Colden. This section of the trail is considered the most breathtaking in the Adirondacks! It passes several lean-tos and then ends at another intersection (5.4 km) — keep right. The route crosses another cross-country ski trail, just before reaching Avalanche Lake (7 km). The towering rocky face of Mount Colden is spectacular. As the trail works its way around the contours of the lake, the little wood bridges it crosses add to the charm.

The trail meets another intersection (8.4 km), keep right towards Algonquin Peak. At the next intersection (9.3 km) continue in the direction of the peak. From here on it is important to pace yourself, because the uphill grade is constant and requires a sustained effort, especially in bad weather. Beyond the timberline (11 km) follow the cairns and the yellow markers painted on rocks. The view from the summit (11.7 km) is a more than generous reward for the efforts of this hike.

For the descent follow the trail down the other side of the mountain. This is the Van Hoevenberg Trail, outlined above. Once back at the Adirondak Loj parking lot the 18-km loop is completed.

■ **Wright Peak**

Level of difficulty:	⌂⌂
Total distance:	*11.4 km*
Time:	*4 h 30 min*
Change in altitude:	*732 m*
Starting point:	*Adirondak Loj parking lot (see p 190).*

Wright Peak is the 16th-tallest in the Adirondacks, and is actually an extension of Algonquin Peak. This hike is an easier alternative to scaling the summit of Algonquin, it also makes an interesting excursion on the return trip from Algonquin.

Follow Van Hoevenberg Trail to the first intersection (1.6 km). The trail climbs gradually to an intersection with Whale's Tail Notch Ski Trail (1.42 km). Beyond a campsite to the left, the trail comes upon a magnificent little waterfall (640 m).

The trail continues to the main intersection (5 km). Turn left, following the sign for "Wright Peak". The summit is 700 m beyond. Beyond the timberline, cairns indicate the way.

Near the summit is a bronze plaque: a memorial to the four-person crew of a B-47 airplane that crashed there in 1962. It is still possible to see debris from the crash. Return by the same trail.

■ Phelps Mountain

Level of difficulty:	⛰⛰
Total distance:	*14.1 km*
Time:	*5 h 30 min*
Change in altitude:	*604 m*
Starting point:	*Adirondak Loj parking lot (see p 190).*

Phelps Mountain is named in honour of Orson Schofield Phelps, nicknamed "Old Mountain", who cleared the first trail to Mount Marcy.

Follow Van Hoevenberg Trail towards Marcy Dam. Phelps Mountain, Mount Colden, and Algonquin Peak are visible from Marcy Dam (3.7 km).

Heading toward Mount Marcy and beyond Marcy Dam, the trail rises gradually and goes by several lean-tos. Once past the lean-tos, the trail stays relatively flat up to the Phelps intersection (5.2 km).

Head in the direction of Phelps Mountain, the summit of which is only 1.9 km away. The trail rises at a regular grade, interrupted by a few steep sections. At the summit (7 km) the rather imposing view is dominated by Mount Marcy, 4.8 km to the south. Return by the same trail.

■ **Mount Colden**

Level of difficulty:	⋀ ⋀ ⋀
Total distance:	*20 km*
Time:	*8 h*
Change in altitude:	*772 m*
Starting point:	*Adirondak Loj parking lot (see p 190).*

Mount Colden was named in honour of David C. Colden, one of the owners of McIntyre Iron Works. The northwest face is steep and almost bare, and is a favourite spot for rock- and ice-climbers. The view from the top of Mount Colden is spectacular; this is probably the best place to admire Mount Marcy and Algonquin Peak, the two highest summits in the Adirondacks.

Follow Van Hoevenberg Trail to Marcy Dam (3.7 km). Turn right close to the lean-to, onto Avalanche Pass Trail. The trail wends its way alongside Marcy Brook and crosses two small bridges. It passes a lean-to at 4.9 km, crosses another bridge, and arrives at the lean-tos of Avalanche Camp (5.4 km).

Just after the second lean-to there is an intersection. Take the Lake Arnold Trail on the left. This trail climbs steadily, crosses a small bridge and reaches another intersection (7 km). Keep right; the trail runs alongside a brook, and up to Lake Arnold and another intersection beside an old lean-to site (7.8 km).

Turn right onto L. Morgan Porter Trail which, leads to the summit of Mount Colden. This trail is alternately flat and steep. It opens up on the northern summit of Mount Colden (9.4 km) and offers a beautiful view. To reach the main summit, follow the trail that leads down and then ascend again. This section is not well marked, so extra attention is required. The summit of Mount Colden is reached after 10 km.

From this mountaintop the real magic of the Adirondacks unfolds before your eyes. On a clear day the summits of Mount Marcy to the southeast, and Algonquin Peak to the northwest are discernible in all their glory! Return by the same trail.

Variations: This hike can be split into two days by spending the night at the Avalanche Camp lean-tos (5.4 km) or by camping at the old lean-to site by Lake Arnold (7.8 km).

It is possible to make a loop by following the same route up and, once at the summit, descending toward Lake Colden and returning by Avalanche Pass Trail. This trail is considered the most impressive of the Adirondacks. The steep descent to Lake Colden makes this 22-km loop very difficult.

■ **Owl's Head Mountain**

Level of difficulty:	
Total distance:	*1.9 km*
Time:	*1 hour*
Change in altitude:	*410 m*
Starting point:	*Small parking lot on Route 73, 5 km west of the village of Keene. On the left (south) side of Route 73, there is a sign for "Owls Head Acres". Take this little road until you reach a sharp right turn, where another road branches off to the left. Keep your eyes peeled; the trail starts in the curve, a little to the left (in spring 1996, there was no sign).*

Owl's Head is a very pleasant little mountain with all the ingredients for a terrific hike: a pretty trail that climbs gradually, a magnificent forest and fantastic views from the summit. All this in less than 1 km! Not surprisingly, it didn't take long for this to hike to become a favourite, especially for young children.

Short but rarely flat, the trail leads up the mountain through a beautiful wooded area. Over the years, the path has been somewhat modified, since it lies almost entirely on private property. Toward the end, it runs along the north side of the mountain, then reaches the rocky, partially bare summit (646 m). The view is outstanding. Cascade Mountain (1,249 m) and Pitchoff Mountain (1,097 m) are easy to spot to the west. If you walk around a bit, you can view the region from different angles and admire Giant Mountain (1,410 m), the 12th highest peak in the Adirondacks, and Mount Hurricane (1,126 m). Return by the same trail.

■ **Pitchoff Mountain**

Level of difficulty:	
Total distance:	*6.4 km*
Time:	*3 hours*
Change in altitude:	*439 m*
Starting point:	*the parking lot for Cascade Mountain, along Route 73, 10.9 km from Keene and 7.2 km from the beginning of Adirondak Loj Road.*

Pitchoff Mountain, located on the north side of Route 73, actually has five summits. Although some hikers explore all five on their way over the mountain (see below), many opt for a shorter outing. In both cases, the view of the neighbouring lakes and mountains is outstanding.

The trail climbs gradually from the start, then veers off to the right on its way to two lookouts, one right after the other (1.3 km). The view of Upper and Lower Cascade Lakes is already ample reward for your efforts, but press on.

The trail continues to climb, sometimes quite steeply, leading to an intersection (2.4 km) at the top of a ridge. The short trail on the right opens onto a wide ledge made up of balanced rocks. After the intersection, the main trail climbs continuously on its way to the summit (3.2 km) of Pitchoff Mountain (1,097 m), from which the view is positively magnificent. Return by the same trail.

Variation: From the first summit, the trail continues to three others, heads down to a pass, then climbs back up to the fifth and final summit. All these summits are exposed, affording some stunning views of the region. From the fifth summit, the trail leads straight down to a parking lot on Route 73, about 4.4 km from the other lot. This 12.3 km loop makes for a fairly difficult hike, but has the advantage of covering varied terrain. You'll also bump into fewer people than on some of the more popular trails.

■ **Cascade Mountain**

Level of difficulty:	
Total distance:	*7.4 km*
Time:	*3 h 30 min*
Change in altitude:	*591 m*

Starting point: parking lot on Route 73, 10.9 km from
                                       Keene, or 7.2 km from the entrance to
                                       Adirondak Loj Road.

Cascade Mountain is so named because of its proximity to Lower and
Upper Cascade Lakes along Route 73. It is the most accessible 1,200-
m-plus mountains in the Adirondacks since it is only 3.8 km from the
parking lot.

From the parking lot the trail starts off downhill for a bit and then begins
to climb steadily. It is not very long, but it ascends at a fairly constant
rate. It continues uninterrupted up to a rocky spur from which the view
is spectacular. Continue to an intersection (3.4 km); the left fork is the
trail leading to Porter Mountain.

To reach the rocky, bare summit of Cascade Mountain continue straight
from the intersection. The summit (3.8 km) offers a splendid, 360° view
of the high peaks (Marcy, Algonquin, Haystack, Giant, etc.), the village
of Lake Placid, and Route 73. Return by the same trail.

Variation: On the return from Cascade Mountain follow the trail from the
intersection leading to Porter Mountain (1,237 m). Hike to the summit
and then back to the intersection. This detour adds 2.2 km to the total
distance, making it 9.6 km return from the parking lot.

■ Crow Mountains

Level of difficulty:
Total distance: 5.6 km loop
Time: 2 h 30 min
Change in altitude: 334 m
Starting point: From the village of Keene, take East Hill
                                       Road for 3.2 km. There is a sign for the trail
                                       on the left side of the road.

The Crow Mountains are two separate summits, Little Crow (747 m)
and Big Crow (858 m). Both, and the latter in particular, offer a truly
magnificent view of the Adirondacks, especially in springtime, when the
highest mountains are still capped with snow.

As the first part of the trail leads through private property, hikers should
take care to respect all regulations (no camping, no fires, etc.). The trail

climbs gradually, passes near a rocky escarpment, then intersects with another trail. The trail leading to the left is an alternative route leading up the west side of the mountain, but it is poorly marked. For that matter, even the main trail is not that well marked and gets confusing in a couple of places. In case of doubt, don't hesitate to retrace your steps to make sure you're on the right path.

Continue along the main trail, which becomes steeper on its way to a pretty scenic viewpoint (0.9 km). It then leads to the western summit of Little Crow, then on to the mountain's main summit (1.4 km; 747 m), which offers an absolutely remarkable view of the valley and the region's many towering mountains.

From the summit of Little Crow, the trail heads down to the pass between the two Crow Mountains (1.8 m) then starts climbing again, this time to the top of Big Crow (2.2 km). Although Big Crow (858 m) is not one of the 100 highest mountains in the Adirondacks, you can still see over 25 lofty peaks from its rocky summit.

The trail then leads down to an intersection (2.6 km). The path on the left leads to the Nun-dagao ridge, and the main trail continues down to Crow Clearing (3.4 km), at the end of a road accessible to cars. Follow this little road 1.9 km to East Hill Road (5.3 km) and turn right to reach the parking lot (5.6 km).

■ **Hurricane Mountain**

Level of difficulty:	🏔🏔
Total distance:	*8.5 km*
Time:	*4 hours*
Change in altitude:	*610 m*
Starting point:	*on Route 9N, 5.8 km to the east of the intersection of Routes 9N and 73, between Keene and Keene Valley. From Elizabethtown, 10.9 km west of the intersection of Routes 9 and 9N.*

The summit of Hurricane Mountain was used for many years as a firefighting base, complete with an observation tower. The base was ideally located since the peak offers a view of most of the high mountains of the Adirondacks, of Lake Champlain, and even of the Green Mountains of Vermont.

Many trails lead to the summit of Hurricane Mountain. The one suggested here is the most popular. It climbs quickly at first and then becomes more moderate and level. The section just before the ridge is quite steep. At the intersection (4 km) turn right, the summit is 250 m ahead (4.2 km). The view is superb from the summit. Return by the same trail.

■ **Baxter Mountain**

Level of difficulty:	
Total distance:	*3.5 km*
Time:	*1 h 30 min*
Change in altitude:	*235 m*
Starting point:	*on Route 9N, 3.2 km from the intersection of Routes 9N and 73 (between Keene and Keene Valley). The trail begins opposite Hurricane Road.*

This is a little mountain, with a short and relatively easy trail, that offers a spectacular view. Of the three trails to the summit the one suggested here is the shortest and easiest. It rises very gradually to the first intersection (1 km). Turn right. The trail is on a slightly steeper incline for the remaining section, to the southeast summit (1.5 km) of Baxter Mountain.

The trail dips down before reaching the higher (744 m) northwest peak of Baxter Mountain (1.7 km). The view from on high encompasses Keene Valley, the Great Range, and, to the southwest, mighty Mount Marcy (1,629 m), the highest mountain in the state of New York. Return by the same trail.

Variation: A loop is possible, but you need to park on the other side of Baxter Mountain, near Beede Farm, in Keene Valley. The tour is 5.23 km in total.

■ **Little Porter Mountain**

Level of difficulty:	
Total distance:	*6.4 km*
Time:	*2 h 45 min*
Change in altitude:	*386 m*

Starting point: *Garden Parking Lot, to the west of the village of Keene Valley (see p 192).*

Little Porter Mountain is the little brother of magnificent Porter Mountain (1,237 m), located farther north, near Cascade Mountain. The trail leading up Little Porter Mountain is relatively short, but has a few steep sections.

From the Garden parking lot, double back along Interbrook Road for about 0.5 km to reach the beginning of the trail, since there is no parking lot there. The trail follows a small road, then leads over a stream and climbs up to an old campground and a private road for all-terrain vehicles (2.2 km). After the road, the trail climbs up to a ridge and intersects with another private road (3.2 km), then follows the mountain ridge to the summit of Little Porter Mountain (3.7 km), which offers an excellent view of the area. Return by the same trail.

Variation: From the top of Little Porter Mountain, continue along the same trail until you reach an intersection. Head left on the Ridge Trail to reach the eastern summit and then the main summit of Porter Mountain, which offers an outstanding 360° view of the region. This variation involves an additional 6.5 km of hiking, doubling the total distance to be covered.

■ **Big Slide Mountain**

Level of difficulty:
Total distance: *12.5 km*
Time: *5 h 30 min*
Change in altitude: *853 m*
Starting point: *Garden parking lot, to the west of Keene Valley.*

The trail proposed here is the shortest but definitely one of the most spectacular. It does not have an official name, but is known as the "Three Brothers" because it encompasses three magnificent vistas from the small summits known as First, Second, and Third Brother. The trip to Second Brother is a short, pleasant hike (5.6 km total).

To the right of the parking lot, take Big Slide Trail, which rises gradually to a view (1.3 km) over Keene Valley. The trail continues to the Brothers. The First Brother is reached at 2.4 km and stands 896 m. The

Second Brother, at 2.7 km, offers superb views to the south, east and west. Nearby is an intersection (2.8 km), and a trail which leads to the "actual" bare summit of Second Brother (950 m).

The trail dips towards the pass between Second and Third Brother, and then ascends Third Brother (4.2 km) for a spectacular view of Big Slide.

The trail descends again and then steepens gradually to an intersection (6 km). Turn right towards the summit of Big Slide. The trail is steep but offers some excellent, open views. From the top of Big Slide (6.3 km), Algonquin Peak, the summit of Giant Mountain, as well as the valley and many other summits are visible. Return by the same trail.

Variation: Make a loop by heading from the summit of Big Slide towards Johns Brook Lodge via Slide Mount Brook Trail. Return to the parking lot by way of Phelps Trail (15.2 km return).

■ Rooster Comb

Level of difficulty:	⛰
Total distance:	*5.6 km*
Time:	*2 h 30 min*
Change in altitude:	*500 m*
Starting point:	*on Interbrook Road (or Johns Brook Road), 1 km west of the sign "Trails to High Peaks", in the centre of Keene Valley.*

The rocky summit of Rooster Comb attracts quite a few hikers. For little toil and trouble the spectacular view is a generous reward. Rooster Comb is not actually a mountain, but rather a shoulder, or continuation, of Hedgehog Mountain.

Follow the road towards Garden parking lot up to the small bridge. Just before the bridge a small sign on the left indicates the way to Rooster Comb and Hedgehog. Park near the bridge since cars are not permitted on the small private road.

From the gate, follow the road to a second gate (700 m), which marks the real beginning of the Rooster Comb trail. Beyond a small bridge over a stream, the trail follows a service road, eventually leaving it (1.3 km) and steepening (2.4 km). The trail finally comes to a spur (2.6 km), from which there is a beautiful view.

The summit of Rooster Comb is an easy 200 m from this spur (2.8 km). A small trail to the right leads to an overhang with another spectacular view of Mount Marcy and Johns Brook Valley. Return by the same trail.

Variation: From the summit of Rooster Comb it is possible to continue up to the summit of Hedgehog Mountain (1,027 m), adding 4.3 km to the trip. The view, however, is not as impressive as that from Rooster Comb.

■ Snow Mountain

Level of difficulty:	
Total distance:	*5.5 km*
Time:	*2 h 30 min*
Change in altitude:	*414 m*
Starting point:	*on Route 73, north of Saint Huberts, after the small Ausable River bridge, 3 km south of the "Trails to High Peaks" sign located in the centre of the village of Keene Valley.*

Snow Mountain is another small summit with an easy hike and great views. Blueberries abound in season. The most popular trail to the summit, the one suggested here, is Deer Brook Trail. The best lookout points are below the crest, on the rocky spurs.

Special attention is necessary because the trail is not always obvious. As well, the trail meets five intersections before reaching the summit (2.8 km). It is helpful to keep in mind that you are heading towards Rooster Comb Trail and Snow Mountain, rather than to the Ausable Club. Return by the same trail.

■ Hopkins Mountain

Mossy Cascade Trail

Level of difficulty:	
Total distance:	*10.2 km*
Time:	*5 hours*
Change in altitude:	*646 m*
Starting point:	*on Route 73, 3.2 km south of Keene Valley, just before Saint Huberts.*

This trail meanders alongside Mossy Cascade Stream for the first kilometre, before arriving at a beautiful, 15-m-high waterfall.

The trail then steepens, providing several pleasant vistas, and heads east towards the last intersection and the crest of Hopkins Mountain (970 m), only a few hundred metres beyond. The view from the summit opens up in almost every direction, and the neighbouring peaks are revealed in all their splendour.

■ **Giant Mountain**

Level of difficulty:	⛰️⛰️
Total distance:	*9.4 km*
Time:	*6 hours*
Change in altitude:	*930 m*
Starting point:	*from the small parking lot on Route 73, 6.6 km north of the junction, at Underwood, of Routes 73 and 9. If the lot is full continue north along the road to the lot at Chapel Pond.*

The first recorded climb of Giant Mountain, which used to be known as "Giant of the Valley", was accomplished in 1797 by Charles Brodhead. The first trail was cleared in 1866.

Many trails lead to the summit, but we suggest Ridge Trail, cleared in 1954. It is the shortest route to the top of the mountain, but also one of the most beautiful and interesting, with many great views along the way.

The trail is rather steep at the beginning. There are three intersections (at 1.1 km, 1.5 km and 1.6 km), the third one with a trail to the summit of Nubble.

Continuing up towards Giant Mountain, traces of a forest fire, which devastated the whole ridge in 1913, are discernable. Paradoxically, the beautiful wide open views along the ridge are actually a result of this disaster.

The trail continues up the rocky slope of the Giant. Quite unexpectedly, there is a small intersection (2.8 km) where a detour skirts a large boulder. The right-hand detour adds 90 m, but the view is much better.

The trail levels off and crosses Roaring Brook Trail (3.5 km). Climbing again, it meets its last intersection, with East Trail (4.5 km) coming from Rocky Peak.

The trail remains fairly flat to the summit (4.7 km), where the view seems to stretch forever over Lake Champlain and the Green Mountains of Vermont to the east, and the 39 high peaks of the Adirondacks to the west. Return by the same trail.

■ Noonmark Mountain

Level of difficulty:	⌃⌃
Total distance:	*10.8 km*
Time:	*5 hours*
Change in altitude:	*578 m*
Starting point:	*little parking lot on Route 73, 1.8 km south of the larger lot at Chapel Pond, and 5 km north of the intersection of Routes 9 and 73. On the topographical map the starting point is marked near Round Pond.*

From Keene Valley the sun is directly over the summit of Noonmark Mountain at noon, hence its name. The trail begins with a gradual slope that continues past Round Pond (900 m) all the way to an intersection at 3.7 km. The summit is 1.6 km further, along a steeper trail that follows the southeast ridge of the mountain.

At the summit of Noonmark Mountain (5.4 km) the view is unobstructed in all directions, revealing the imposing Giant Mountain (1,410 m) to the northeast, Dix Mountain (1,480 m) to the south, and the Great Range to the west. Return by the same trail.

Variation: On the hike down from Noonmark, at the intersection with the trail to Dix Mountain, the left trail leads to the summit of Round Mountain. The return trip to Round Mountain adds 7.6 km to the original route.

■ **Bald Peak**

East Trail

Level of difficulty:	◪ ◪
Total distance:	*12.4 km*
Time:	*5 h 30 min*
Change in altitude:	*740 m*
Starting point:	*parking lot on Route 9, 7.3 km north of Route 73.*

East Trail leads to the summit of Bald Peak (927 m) and is one of the most beautiful hikes in the region, with spectacular views en route.

After 3.2 km the trail arrives at an intersection and a detour leads to a lookout over the valley from the small summit known as Blueberry Cobbles. The trail steepens and then reaches the crest of Bald Peak with its exceptional views in all directions. Return by the same trail.

Variation: With time and energy to spare it is possible to continue to the summit of Giant Mountain (1,410 m), via Rocky Peak Ridge. This route adds 13.4 km to the total distance, making it a very difficult hike.

■ **Gilligan Mountain**

Level of difficulty:	◪
Total distance:	*3.6 km*
Time:	*1 h 30 min*
Change in altitude:	*204 m*
Starting point:	*The entrance to the parking lot is located along Route 9, 5.8 km north of Route 73. A small unpaved road leads to the fisherman's parking, right before the little bridge over the Boquet River. This lot can also be used by hikers.*

Although it is just a little over 400 m high, Gilligan Mountain affords some magnificent panoramas — and little physical effort is required. Located east of the higher peaks, it offers a slightly different view of the Adirondacks than other mountains.

From the parking lot, you have to cross the little bridge and walk about a hundred metres to reach the beginning of the trail, on the left, just before a house. The trail is fairly flat at first, then climbs gradually up to a scenic viewpoint (.5 km), from which you can admire Dix Mountain to the west.

After reaching a second lookout, the trail becomes easier, leading through a little pass and crossing an old forest road. At the third, more open lookout, you can take a little rest (1.4 km). Rocky Peak (1,347 m) and Dix Mountain (1,480 m), the sixth highest summit in the Adirondacks, are easy to spot from here.

The trail then leads to another little forest road, which it follows for a little while before branching off to the left and climbing up to the last and largest scenic viewpoint (1.8 km). The official trail stops here, as the real summit of Gilligan Mountain (433 m), located right nearby, is wooded and doesn't afford a view. Return by the same trail.

■ **Poke-o-moonshine**

Level of difficulty:	
Total distance:	*3.8 km*
Time:	*2 hours*
Change in altitude:	*390 m*
Starting point:	*at the end of the state campground on Route 9. Take Exit 33 off of Interstate 87. Continue along Route 9 South for 4.8 km, until you reach the campground on the right. Park at the campground (fee charged) or 0.4 km farther.*

Poke-O-Moonshine is very popular with climbers from this region, and from elsewhere, who can commonly be seen scaling the face of the mountain, just before the campground. The big slabs of rock on the southeast side are less formidable.

The trail starts at the south end of the campground, not far from the road. It is fairly steep at the beginning, climbing up through the woods. After the first lookout (0.5 km), however, it gets somewhat easier. Near the southern ridge of the mountain (1.3 km), on the left, you'll find a lean-to and the remains of a cabin.

There are two trails leading from the ridge to the mountaintop. Take the one on the left; the one on the right is the old path. The trail climbs along a ledge up to the rocky summit (1.9 km) of Poke-O-Moonshine (664 m), where you'll find an observation tower used for spotting forest fires and enjoy a remarkable view of the region's lofty mountains and Lake Champlain. Return by the same trail.

■ Mount Haystack

Level of difficulty:	◪ ◪
Total distance:	*10.6 km*
Time:	*4 hours*
Change in altitude:	*377 m*
Starting point:	*the big parking lot along Route 86, between the towns of Lake Placid and Ray Brook. If you're coming from Lake Placid, it will be on your right. The trail head is indicated by a sign.*

It would have been easier and clearer to name this mountain "North Haystack" or "Little Haystack", since many hikers mistake it for majestic Haystack Mountain (1,512 m), the third highest summit in the Adirondacks, which rises up proudly southeast of Mount Marcy. Be that as it may, you can enjoy some lovely views from "Little Haystack" without the major exertion.

The difficulty of this trail lies more in its length (10.6 km) than in the change in altitude. It climbs gradually, demanding little effort. The first part heads up the mountain then back down a bit. Next, the trail crosses a small stream, goes a little farther downhill, and leads to a lookout (2.4 km).

Farther along, it links up with the old trail, then follows a small forest road to an intersection (3.9 km).

Turn left at the intersection, at which point the trail becomes the Haystack Trail. After crossing two streams, it gets steeper and leads to a rocky ledge, then up to the summit (5.3 km).

At the top of "Little" Haystack (876 m), you'll be able to drink in some magnificent views of the surrounding area, including three celebrated summits: Whiteface Mountain (1,483 m), Algonquin Peak (1,559 m) and Mount Marcy (1,628 m). Return by the same trail.

■ **Scarface Mountain**

Level of difficulty:	
Total distance:	*10.4 km*
Time:	*4 h 15 min*
Change in altitude:	*450 m*
Starting point:	*along Ray Brook Road, in the village of the same name. From Lake Placid, take Route 86 toward Saranac Lake. At Ray Brook, turn left on Ray Brook Road. Almost immediately after, on the left, you'll see the sign marking the trail head.*

Located just south of the little community of Ray Brook, between the towns of Lake Placid and Saranac Lake, Scarface Mountain (932 m) offers some lovely views of the region.

The first part of the trail is relatively flat and easy to hike. The path then leads across some old railway tracks and a small bridge, climbing up to intersect with an old road (2.4 km). This little road is actually the former trail to Scarface Mountain. Turn left and follow it for about 350 m. The trail then branches off to the left (2.7 km), leads across a small stream, and climbs up to the western ridge of the mountain.

The trail gets steeper on its way up to a pretty lookout (5 km). Farther along, it is more exposed, affording some lovely views to the south (there are a number of small, unmarked trails leading to other, lovely scenic viewpoints). The trail comes to an end at the western summit (5.2 km) of Scarface Mountain, 0.6 km from the eastern summit. Return by the same trail.

■ **Baker Mountain**

Level of difficulty:	
Total distance:	*2.8 km*
Time:	*1 h 30 min*
Change in altitude:	*274 m*

Starting point: *Baker Mountain lies right behind the village of Saranac Lake. From Route 86 in Lake Placid, turn right onto River Road, which forms a big, sharp curve; keep your eyes open for the NBT bank. Right after the railroad tracks, turn left on Pine Street, then continue to East Pine and take a right. After the little bridge, continue straight ahead to the end of Moody Pond, where you'll see a sign for the trail on the left.*

Baker Mountain is very popular with the residents of Saranac Lake, and with good reason; a minimum of physical exertion and hikers are rewarded with a panoramic view of the region, including several magnificent lakes and mountains.

To start out, follow the trail leading to the right, which then veers off to the left, runs near an old quarry, then heads back to the right. It starts climbing more gradually on its way to a Y-shaped intersection (0.9 km), at which point you can take either path, since they connect again farther along. The trail to the right is a little steeper, but the views are prettier.

The two trails merge together (1.3 km) a short distance from the top of the mountain (1.4 km), which is covered with magnificent pine trees. Although the summit (749 m) is wooded, there are some magnificent lookouts, from which you can admire the village of Saranac Lake, a few large lakes and Mount McKenzie (1,168 m) to the east, as well as several lofty summits to the south. Return by the same trail.

■ Ampersand Mountain

Level of difficulty:	⛰⛰
Total distance:	*8.8 km loop*
Time:	*3 h 45 min*
Change in altitude:	*541 m*
Starting point:	*The parking lot is located on the right side of Route 3, near Middle Saranac Lake.*

Ampersand Mountain might not be one of the 100 highest points in the Adirondacks, but it has no cause to envy its loftier neighbours. Thanks to its unique geographic location, northwest of the highest mountains, and its bare summit, it offers a breathtaking view of the region.

The trail starts on the other side of Route 3, just opposite the parking lot. It is fairly flat and leads through a lovely forest. Farther along, the terrain gets damper, especially in the spring, and there are little wooden bridges leading across flooded areas. A number of giant trees have been uprooted, bearing witness to the violent storms that have swept through this region in recent years.

After this relatively flat section, the trail starts getting steeper (1.9 km), then veers off to the right, at which point the hike gets somewhat difficult, due to the erosion of the soil. At the top of the ridge (3.9 km), it is easygoing for a while as the trail leads back downhill for a little while, then heads up to the rocky summit. On the last leg of the trip, it turns right and leads through the rocks to the top of the mountain (4.4 km).

The summit of Ampersand Mountain (1,022 m) is completely exposed, offering a 360° view of the region. Several lakes and a large number of towering mountains are easily identifiable.

This summit was once covered with trees, but many of them were cut down when an observation tower, used to spot forest fires, was built here. Wind, rain and erosion took care of the rest, leaving the mountaintop completely bare. There are no signs left of the observation tower, but a commemorative plaque serves as a reminder of that era. Return by the same trail.

■ **Whiteface Mountain**

Whiteface Mountain is the fifth highest summit in the Adirondacks at 1,483 m. Being 16 km north of any other peak over 1,200 m and 12.8 km from the town of Lake Placid, the view from its beautiful bare summit is unobstructed.

Whiteface Mountain is, however, quite developed. As well as the two hiking trails that criss-cross it, there is a ski resort, a toll-road leading to within 90 m of the summit (from the parking lot to the crest), and a weather station.

The trail recommended here, Wilmington Trail, is the easier of the two.

Trail to Whiteface

Level of difficulty:	⌂⌂⌂
Total distance:	*16.6 km*
Time:	*7 hours*
Change in altitude:	*1,103 m*
Starting point:	*from Exit 34 on Interstate 87, take 9N to the village of Jay. From Jay take Route 86 to Wilmington. At the end of the village, on a curve, take the Whiteface Memorial Highway (431) 0.8 km to the sign on the left, Trail to Whiteface.*

Follow this road for 0.4 km, to the parking lot. From the parking lot the trail leads to an intersection (3.5 km) with the path to Marble Mountain whose summit is only 140 m to the right. This small mountain was a ski centre until 1956. To the left the trail continues and soon reveals the summit of Esther Mountain (1,292 m).

The trail becomes progressively rougher. A bit further along (5.4 km) it emerges onto a beautiful vista of the summit of Whiteface. The trail descends again before climbing to a lean-to (7.2 km).

The trail winds alongside the road to the timberline, at 7.8 km. The remainder of the trail is spectacular. It passes left of the Summit Building and then up to the mountaintop (8.3 km). Return by the same trail.

Variation: It is possible to make this a two-day hike by staying overnight at the lean-to (7.2 km).

■ **Catamount Mountain**

Level of difficulty:	⌂
Total distance:	*5.8 km*
Time:	*2 h 45 min*
Change in altitude:	*466 m*

Starting point:

along Forestdale Road. From the village of Ausable Forks, take Silver Lake Road towards Silver Lake and Black Brook, then head left on Nelson Road. At Forestdale Road, turn left again, then continue for about 8 km to the beginning of the trail, located on the right side of the road, before the big fields and houses. Keep your eyes peeled; the trail leads right to the road, but there is no sign for it.

Catamount Mountain is located directly north of magnificent Whiteface Mountain. It is a small mountain (966 m) with two summits which offer a truly intoxicating view of the region. In fact, Catamount Mountain is considered one of the most wonderful little mountains in the Adirondacks; not only does it offer spectacular views, but the trail leading up it is short, varied and thrilling.

The first part of the trail is fairly flat and winds through a young forest full of little conifers. This part of the trail is marked with orange paint. After 0.9 km, however, you have to head off to the right, into unmarked territory. The trail becomes somewhat more difficult at this point, as it leads into a magnificent birch forest.

The trail crosses a small stream (1.3 km) and runs past a series of burnt trees, getting steeper and steeper along the way. To reach the first summit, you have to climb over some boulders and pass through a small rock chimney. This summit (2.4 km) offers a view of both the valley and the main summit.

The trail then leads through the wooded pass between the two summits and climbs straight up to the main summit, following a series of little cairns. The views from the top (2.9 km; 966 m) of Catamount Mountain are sublime. To the south, Whiteface Mountain (1,483 m), the fifth highest point in the Adirondacks, rises up in all its majesty; to the north, you can admire Taylor and Silver Lakes. Return by the same trail.

■ **Silver Lake**

Level of difficulty:
Total distance: *3 km*
Time: *1 h 30 min*

Change in altitude:	*275 m*
Starting point:	*The parking lot is located along Silver Lake Road. From Interstate 87, take Route 9N to the village of Ausable Forks and turn right at the blinking red light. At the next stop, turn left toward Silver Lake and Black Brook. After the little sign for the village of Hawkeye, where you can enjoy a perfect view of Silver Lake Mountain, you'll see a brown sign marking the beginning of the trail on the right.*

Silver Lake Mountain is very small (724 m) but affords some lovely views. The trail leading up it is short, well cleared and easy. Furthermore, it winds through a magnificent pine forest, which carpets the path in wonderfully fragrant pine needles.

You can admire the region from two lookouts (0.8 km and 1.1 km) along the way, while the summit (1.5 km) offers a very attractive view of majestic Whiteface Mountain (1,483 m), the fifth highest point in the Adirondacks, as well as Silver and Taylor Lakes. Actually, the real summit of the mountain, which is wooded, is located some 500 m farther. The top of Silver Lake Mountain forms a rocky ridge over 3 km long. The little trail that runs along it, however, is neither marked nor maintained. Return by the same trail.

 Long Hikes

■ Mount Marcy

Mount Marcy is a lot of mountain — at 1,629 m, it is the tallest peak in the Adirondacks! Its rounded summit attracts thousands of hikers each year. The mountain was named after Governor William Learned Marcy by Ebenezer Emmons, a chemistry professor at Williams College. Emmons first ascended its peak on August 5th, 1837, accompanied by his son, Ebenezer Jr., and a group of explorers. Long before this, however, the native people of the area had climbed the mountain and called it Tahawus, "the mountain that parts the clouds".

The first trail to the peak was cleared in 1861. It begins near Upper Ausable Lake. Once at the summit, an incredible unobstructed view unfolds in every direction, making it possible to identify 43 of the 45 high mountains of the Adirondacks.

To the east-northeast over Gothics, it is even possible, if the sky is clear, to distinguish the unique outline of Camel's Hump, 86 km away in the Green Mountains of Vermont!

Below Mount Marcy on the northern side is the village of Lake Placid, site of the 1932 and 1980 Winter Olympics. Even the ski-jump is visible. Lake Placid stretches out behind the village, and northeast of it, on the right, is majestic Whiteface Mountain (1,483 m), an important downhill ski resort and the fifth-highest summit in the Adirondacks.

Many trails lead to the summit of Mount Marcy, but unfortunately no short or easy ones. The two suggested here are the most picturesque and popular routes.

Van Hoevenberg Trail

Level of difficulty:	⚑ ⚑ ⚑
Total distance:	*23.6 km*
Time:	*2 days*
Change in altitude:	*965 m*
Starting point:	*Adirondak Loj parking lot (see p 190).*

From the town of Keene, take Route 73 West 18 km towards Lake Placid. A sign on the left indicates the entrance to Adirondak Loj. This small 7.7-km-long road leads directly to the parking lot. If you are coming from Lake Placid, the sign is 6.4 km from the village on the right.

Van Hoevenberg Trail is named after Henry Van Hoevenberg, who built the Adirondack Lodge in the 1880's. Adirondack Lodge is an inn, and is distinct from Adirondak Loj, which is a shelter for campers and hikers. The Van Hoevenberg Trail is a very steady uphill trail, so steady that in winter it allows cross-country skiers access to the summit of Mount Marcy.

The trail starts out relatively flat, crossing the trail to Algonquin Peak at 1.6 km. Continue in the direction of Mount Marcy and Marcy Dam (3.7 km), where weather permitting, you can see Phelps Mountain, Mount Colden, and Algonquin Peak. There are seven lean-tos, and many campsites, located close to Marcy Dam. On the southeast wall of the dam, drinking water flows from a pipe.

Beyond the dam, the Van Hoevenberg Trail crosses Avalanche Pass Trail. It climbs gradually and then flattens out to the Phelps intersection (5.2 km). A bit further along a small bridge straddles Phelps Stream. The trail then crosses a few cross-country ski trails and get quite steep as it climbs to a lookout, at 6.9 km, with a view of Mount Marcy. Nearby, just before Indian Falls (7 km), is the campground.

Before setting up camp it is best to plan the rest of the hike. This will depend on the weather, the time, and the level of fatigue of the hikers. There are two options:

• Hike to the summit with just a small day-pack and return to the campsite at Indian Falls (9.4 km return) for dinner and the night. The following day return to the starting point.

    Day One: 16.5 km   Day Two: 7 km

• Sleep at Indian Falls. The next day rise early, and hike to the summit with a small day-pack. Return to Indian Falls, retrieve your camping gear, and then hike back to the starting point.

    Day One: 7 km   Day Two: 16.5 km

From Indian Falls, the route continues steadily up to, and beyond, the intersection with the trail from Keene Valley (2.8 km). There are a number of spectacular views of Mount Marcy along the way. The trail meets another intersection at 3.8 km and then winds along Mount Marcy's rocky shoulder; pay close attention to the cairns and to the yellow markers painted on the ground and on large rocks, especially in bad weather or in fog as there are many loose rocks and cliffs in this area.

The view is breathtaking at the summit (4.7 km). It is quite a sensation to be at the top of this pinnacle, with the state of New York stretched out at your feet!

Variation: It is possible to hike to the summit and back in one day. This hike of 23.62 km is, however, extremely long and should only be attempted by experienced hikers, for whom eight hours of fast walking poses no problem. This is a very difficult hike and requires a very early start.

Trail to the High Peak

Level of difficulty:	⌂⌂⌂
Total distance:	*29.1 km*
Time:	*2 days*
Change in altitude:	*1,165 m*
Starting point:	*Garden parking lot, west of Keene Valley (see p 192).*

From Keene, take route 73 towards Keene Valley. In the centre of Keene Valley, near the sign "Trail to the High Peaks", take Interbrook Road to the parking lot (2.6 km from the sign). The lot can accommodate 60 cars.

Day One: The trail is relatively flat as it follows the valley floor. Head in the direction of Johns Brook Lodge, which is an easy 5.6 km along the trail. From there, follow Phelps Trail which leads to an intersection immediately following the first lean-to at Bushnell Falls — turn left (the markers from here on are red). The trail passes several lean-tos and later crosses a small stream (10.2 km). Further along, the trail arrives at the Slant Rock (10.9 km), the campsite for the night.

Day Two: Just beyond the shelter, the trail comes to another intersection (11 km). It is steeper and more difficult up to the next junction (12.5 km), called Panter Gorge. This marks the halfway point between Mount Marcy and Haystack. Turn right, towards the last intersection at 13.5 km. The trail now follows Mount Marcy's rocky ridge, it is therefore important to follow the cairns and yellow markers painted on rocks and on the ground. In bad weather or in fog, be particularly careful to stay on the trail — there are many loose rocks and cliffs along this section. The view from the summit (14.5 km) is exceptional.

The return is via the same trail — from the summit down to Slant Rock, then towards Johns Brook Lodge and Garden parking lot.

Depending on weather conditions, time and your energy level, it is possible to continue up to the summit on the first day, after setting up camp, and return to the lean-to for the night. Day Two would be relatively short, comprising only the hike down to the parking lot (10.9 km).

Day One: 10.9 km or Day One: 18 km
Day Two: 18 km or Day Two: 10.9 km

■ Haystack Mountain

Level of difficulty:	⛰️⛰️⛰️
Total distance:	*28.5 km*
Time:	*2 days*
Change in altitude:	*1,048 m*
Starting point:	*Garden parking lot west of Keene Valley (see p 192).*

Haystack Mountain is the third highest mountain in the Adirondacks, measuring in at 1,512 m. The honour of its first ascent is attributed to Mr. O.S. Phelps who climbed it with two friends in 1849. He remarked that the bare summit resembled a haystack, and the name stuck.

Those looking for an impressive mountain, and who have a taste for solitude will be satisfied on both counts here. Haystack is located just east-southeast of Mount Marcy, and many hikers overlook it in favour of the larger Mount Marcy. As a result, Haystack, along with Skylight, is one of the least travelled of the region's high peaks.

There are many routes up to the summit of Haystack. The trail suggested here takes two days and passes by Johns Brook Lodge.

Day One: The trail is relatively flat as it follows the valley floor. Head in the direction of Johns Brook Lodge, which is an easy 5.6 km along the trail. From there, follow Phelps Trail which leads to an intersection immediately following the first lean-to at Bushnell Falls — turn left (the markers from here on are red). The trail passes several lean-tos and later crosses a small stream (10.2 km). Further along, the trail arrives at Slant Rock (10.9 km), the campsite for the night.

Day Two: Get up early, prepare a light day-pack, and follow Range Trail, indicated by yellow markers. At the first intersection head towards Little Haystack, and then towards Haystack itself.

From the lean-to at Slant Rock it is important to pay attention to the trail, because the route is not always clear. Be careful not to end up heading toward Mount Marcy. It is 3.3 km from the lean-to at Slant Rock to the summit of Haystack. You will have to leave early because the day includes the hike to the summit and back, retrieval of your gear at Slant Rock, and the hike back down to the Garden parking lot. Depending on the weather, time, and your level of fatigue, days one and two may be reversed.

Day One: 10.9 km or Day One: 17.6 km
Day Two: 17.6 km or Day Two: 10.9 km

■ Dix Mountain

Level of difficulty:	◣◣◣
Total distance:	*21.9 km*
Time:	*2 days*
Change in altitude:	*975 m*
Starting point:	*small parking lot on Route 73, 1.8 km south of the larger lot at Chapel Pond. It is 5 km north of the intersection of Routes 9 and 73. On the topographical map the starting point is indicated next to Round Pond.*

Ebenezer Emmons named Dix Mountain, in 1837, in honour of John A. Dix, Governor of New York State and Major General in the armed forces. The first non-native man to climb it, however, was a Mr. Rykert in 1807.

The trail rises gradually to Round Pond (900 m), and goes beyond it to the intersection (3.7 km) of Old Dix Trail and Felix Adler Trail, which leads to the summit of Noonmark. Take the trail to the left, which flattens out, follows a small stream, and then gently climbs to Boquet River lean-to, the campsite for the night.

At this point, you have two options, depending on the weather, time, and level of fatigue of the hikers. Either continue up to the summit with a light day-pack, after setting up camp, and then return to spend the night at the lean-to, or get an early start the next morning, hike to the summit with a light day-pack, and dismantle the camp on the return to the starting point.

Day One: 6.8 km or Day One: 15 km
Day Two: 15 km or Day Two: 6.8 km

From the shelter to the summit the trail is very steep. At one point there is a change in altitude of 490 m over 1.6 km! The trail intersects Hunter's Pass Trail (10.3 km); turn left for the summit of Dix. In an effort to protect the fragile vegetation pay attention to the trail markers. The view from the summit (10.9 km) is 360° of unobstructed splendour! To the east are Lake Champlain and the Green Mountains of Vermont. The return is by the same trail, given that you will have to retrieve your gear at the lean-to.

Variation: It is possible to hike up the southwest side of Dix Mountain, via Beckhorn, making a return trip of 21 km from the starting point at Lake Elk parking lot.

■ **Gothics**

Level of difficulty:	⌂⌂
Total distance:	*21.8 km*
Time:	*2 days*
Change in altitude:	*910 m*
Starting point:	*Garden Parking lot behind Keene Valley.*

From the parking lot head towards the DEC Interior Outpost (5 km), located just before Johns Brook Lodge. At the intersection take Orebed Brook Trail. Pay close attention to the route, because many trails intersect on this 900 metre stretch.

Gothics is the tenth highest summit in the Adirondacks. Its steep rocky peak rarely fails to make an impression. Steel cables providing assistance for the final magnificent climb. Frederick Perkins and Mr. Phelps coined the name "Gothics" in 1857, when they spied this mountain's rocky summit from atop Mount Marcy and decided it resembled Gothic architecture.

The trail climbs at a moderate pace and arrives at Orebed Lean-To, the campsite for the night (on the left at 7 km). Tents may be set up next to the lean-to. Depending on weather conditions, the time, and your level of fatigue, the hike to the summit of Gothics may be accomplished on the first day or the next morning.

Day One: 7 km or Day One: 14.8 km
Day Two: 14.8 km or Day Two: 7 km

From Orebed Lean-To to the summit of Gothics

The trail beyond Orebed Lean-To is relatively flat at the beginning, but eventually steepens, quite sharply in certain spots. Near the intersection, there are a few spectacular lookout points. At the intersection with the State Range Trail (9.9 km), which leads to Saddleback, head towards Gothics Mountain. This last kilometre is a hiker's paradise!

Follow the markers painted on rocks and use the steel cables as supports. These are helpful in bad weather. Beyond the two cables is the first summit (10.7 km), with a superb view. There is, however, one more intersection to cross before reaching the true summit of Gothics Mountain (10.9 km). The view from this peak is unobstructed in every direction, permitting identification of more than 30 of the high peaks of the region. Return by the same trail.

Variations: With extra time you could also climb to the summit of Saddleback on the way down from Gothics. From the intersection it is 900 m (one way) to the summit.

It is possible to hike to the top of Gothics and back in one day. This 21.8 km hike then becomes very difficult.

Answers to true-false quiz p 12.

1. False	16. False
2. True	17. False
3. True	18. True
4. False	19. False
5. True	20. True
6. True	21. True
7. False	22. False
8. True	23. False
9. True	24. False
10. False	25. True
11. True	26. True
12. False	27. False
13. False	28. False
14. False	29. True
15. True	30. True

Summary Charts of Hikes

■ **Vermont**

MOUNT MANSFIELD REGION	Level of difficulty	Total distance (km)	Time	Change of altitude (m)	Page
SHORT HIKES					
Mount Mansfield: Haselton Trail	‹	6.8	4 h	780	78
Mount Mansfield: Sunset Ridge	‹	10.6	4 h 30	622	78
Mount Mansfield: Laura Cowles	‹ ‹	8.6	5 h	622	79
Mount Mansfield: Halfway House	‹	8	4 h	470	80
Mount Mansfield: Butler Lodge	‹	7.2	5 h 30	774	79
Mount Mansfield: Maple Ridge Trail	‹	8.3	5 h	777	84
Mount Mansfield: Long Trail	‹	7.4	5 h 15	850	81
Mount Mansfield: Subway	‹ ‹	.5 (one-way)	15 min	100	80
Mount Mansfield: Tundra Trail	‹	4.2	1 h 15	165	81
Mount Mansfield: Hell Brook Trail	‹ ‹	8	5 h 30	792	83
Spruce Peak: Elephant's Head	‹	7.8	3 h	457	85
Mount Hunger	‹	6.2	3 h 30	706	86
Stowe Pinnacle	‹	4.6	2 h 30	463	87
LONG HIKES					
Mount Mansfield: Long Trail	‹	17.8	2 days	622	88
Mount Mansfield: Loop from Underhill State Camping Area	‹	9.9	2 days	622	89

CAMEL'S HUMP REGION	Level of difficulty	Total distance (km)	Time	Change of altitude (m)	Page
SHORT HIKES					
Camel's Hump: Camel's Hump View Trail	‹	1.3	45 min	806	93
Camel's Hump: Eastern Loop	‹‹	12	6 h	806	93
Camel's Hump: Western Loop	‹‹	9	5 h	665	95
Green Mountain Audubon Nature Center	‹	total 8	15 min - 1 h	max 60	96

CENTRAL VERMONT REGION	Level of difficulty	Total distance (km)	Time	Change of altitude (m)	Page
SHORT HIKES					
Mount Abraham	‹	8.4	4 h	482	97
Texas Falls		1.9	1 h	50	98
Robert Frost Trail		1.6	1 h	35 m	99
Mount Horrid		2.4	1 h	188	100
Falls of Lana	‹	1.8	1 h	75	101

KILLINGTON PEAK REGION

	Level of difficulty	Total distance (km)	Time	Change of altitude (m)	Page
SHORT HIKES					
Killington Peak	⋀⋀	11.6	5 h 30	755	103
Pico Peak	⋀⋀	9.2	4 h	550	105
Deer Leap Mountain	⋀	5.6	2 h	240	106
Blue Ridge Mountain	⋀	7.8	3 h 30	454	107

LAKE WILLOUGHBY REGION

	Level of difficulty	Total distance (km)	Time	Change of altitude (m)	Page
SHORT HIKES					
Mount Pisgah	⋀	6.2	2 h 30	442	108
Mount Hor	⋀	5.4	2 h 30	320	110
Bald Mountain	⋀⋀	6.8	2 h 45	442	111
Haystack Mountain	⋀	3.2	1 h 30	266	112
Wheeler Mountain	⋀	3.6	1 h 45	210	113

■ **New Hampshire**

FRANCONIA NOTCH REGION	Level of difficulty	Total distance (km)	Time	Change of altitude (m)	Page
SHORT HIKES					
Artist's Bluff and Bald Mountain	◄	2.4	1 h 15	120	120
Mounts Lincoln and Lafayette	◄◄	14.5	7 h 30	1143	121
Mounts Flume and Liberty	◄◄	16	8 h	1026	123
The Flume	◄	3.2	1 h 15	120	124
Mount Pemigewasset	◄	5.8	2 h 30	356	125

KANCAMAGUS HIGHWAY	Level of difficulty	Total distance (km)	Time	Change of altitude (m)	Page
SHORT HIKES					
Sabbaday Falls	◄	1.2	30 min	30	127
Russell-Colbath Historic Site	◄	0.8	15 min	-	127
Champney Falls	◄	5.6	2 h	210	128
Boulder Loop Trail	◄	5	2 h 30	275	129

CRAWFORD NOTCH REGION	Level of difficulty	Total distance (km)	Time	Change of altitude (m)	Page
SHORT HIKES					
Mount Willard	◄	5.2	2 h	285	131
Mount Crawford	◄◄	8	4 h 30	640	132

MOUNT WASHINGTON REGION	Level of difficulty	Total distance (km)	Time	Change of altitude (m)	Page
SHORT HIKES					
Boy Mountain	≺	2.2	1 h	209	143
Mount Starr King	≺≺	9	4 h	735	144
Mount Adams: Air Line and Valley Way Trails	≺≺ ≺	14.5	7 h 30	1370	145
Mount Adams: Lowe's Path Trail	≺≺ ≺	15.4	7 h 30	1300	146
Mount Jefferson: Caps Ridge Trail	≺≺ ≺	8	4 h	824	146
Mount Jefferson: Castle Trail	≺≺ ≺	16.2	8 h	1310	147
Mount Eisenhower	≺≺ ≺	10.6	5 h	830	148
Slide Peak: Glen Boulder Trail	≺	8.4	4 h 30	850	149
Mount Jackson: Webster–Jackson Trail		8.6	4 h 30	652	149
Pine Mountain: Ledge Trail	≺	5.2	2 h	228	150
Mount Washington: Tuckerman Ravine Trail	≺≺ ≺	13.5	7 h	1306	150
Mount Washington: Lion Head Trail	≺≺ ≺	5	2 h 45	786	151
Mount Washington: Huntington Ravine Trail	≺≺ ≺	13.8	8 h	1306	151
Boott Spur Trail	≺≺ ≺	17.4	8 h	786	152
Alpine Garden Trail	≺	1.9	45 min	30	153
Ammonoosuc Ravine Trail	≺≺	12.4	7 h	1192	153
Mount Madison: Osgood Trail	≺	18	7 h	1178	154
LONG HIKES					
The Great Gulf	≺≺	21.4	2 days	1306	154
Crossing the Presidential Range (first option)	≺≺	29	3 days	1306	155
Crossing the Presidential Range (second option)	≺	32.8	3 days	1060	156

■ Maine

BAXTER PARK	Level of difficulty	Total distance (km)	Time	Change of altitude (m)	Page
SHORT HIKES					
South Turner Mountain	‹‹	6.4	3 h	500	164
Sentinel Mountain	‹‹	9.6	4 h	250	164
Mount Coe	‹‹‹	10.6	6 h	775	165
North Brother Mountain	‹‹‹	12	6 h	890	165
Owl Mountain	‹‹	10.6	4 h 30	780	166
Doubletop Mountain	‹‹‹	10.6	5 h	720	166
Mount Katahdin: Hunt Trail	‹‹‹‹	16.8	8 h 30	1245	168
Mount Katahdin: Abol Trail	‹‹‹‹	14.5	9 h	1216	169
Mount Katahdin: Baxter Peak	‹‹‹‹	13.8	8 h 30	1147	169
Mount Katahdin: Knife Edge	‹‹	1.8	2 h	110	170
Mount Katahdin: Chimney Pond Trail	‹‹	5.3	2 h	430	171
Mount Katahdin: Hamlin Peak	‹‹‹‹	14.4	7 h	990	171
Mount Katahdin: Dudley Trail	‹‹‹‹	3.9	4 h	727	172
Mount Katahdin: Cathedral Trail	‹‹	2.6	2 h 30	727	173
Mount Katahdin: Saddle Trail	‹‹	3.5	2 h	727	173

ACADIA NATIONAL PARK	Level of difficulty	Total distance (km)	Time	Change of altitude (m)	Page
SHORT HIKES					
Beech Mountain Trail	◄	2.9	1 h 15	100	179
Great Head Trail	◄	2	45 min	40	179
Ocean Trail	◄	5.8	2 h	-	179
Ship Harbor	◄	1.5	45 min	-	180
Mount Champlain: Precipice Trail	◄◄	1.3	1 h 15	300	180
Mount Champlain: Beachcroft Trail	◄◄	2.6	1 h 45	300	181
Mount Champlain: Beehive Trail	◄◄	1.9	45 min	150	181
Gorham Mountain	◄◄	3.2	1 h 15	150	181
Dorr Mountain	◄◄	4.8	2 h 15	363	182
Cadillac Mountain: Cadillac Mountain South Ridge Trail	◄◄	11.2	4 h 30	424	182
Cadillac Mountain: Cadillac West Face Trail	◄	4.6	2 h 30	335	183
Pemetic Mountain: Pemetic Mountain Trail		6.4	2 h 30	292	183
Pemetic Mountain: Bubble-Pemetic Trail		1.6	1 h	267	184
Penobscot Mountain: Jordan Cliffs Trail	◄◄	5.4	2 h 15	278	184
Penobscot Mountain: Penobscot Mountain Trail	◄	4.8	2 h	278	184
Acadia Mountain: Acadia Mountain Trail	◄	3.2	1 h 15	176	185
Mount St. Sauveur: Ledge Trail	◄	2.6	1 h 10	145	185
Flying Mountain: Flying Mountain Trail	◄	1	30 min	86	186

■ **New York**

ADIRONDACKS	Level of difficulty	Total distance (km)	Time	Change of altitude (m)	Page
SHORT HIKES					
Mount Jo	<	3.7	1 h 30	212	195
Mount Van Hoevenberg	<	7	2 h 45	225	196
Rocky Falls	<	7.7	2 h 30	-	197
Algonquin Peak: Van Hoevenberg Trail	< <	12.8	6 h 30	895	198
Algonquin Peak : Avalanche Pass Trail	< <	18.1	8 h	895	198
Wright Peak	< <	11.4	4 h 30	732	199
Phelps Mountain	< <	14.1	5 h 30	604	200
Mount Colden	< <	20	8 h	772	201
Owls Head Mountain	<	1.9	1 h	410	202
Pitchoff Mountain	<	6.4	3 h	439	203
Cascade Mountain	<	7.4	3 h 30	591	203
Crow Mountains	<	5.6	2 h 30	334	204
Hurricane Mountain	<	8.5	4 h	610	205
Baxter Mountain	<	3.5	1 h 30	235	206
Little Porter Mountain	<	6.4	2 h 45	386	206
Big Slide Mountain	<	12.5	5 h 30	853	207
Rooster Comb	<	5.6	2 h 30	500	208
Snow Mountain	<	5.5	2 h 30	414	209
Hopkins Mountain: Mossy Cascade Trail	<	10.2	5 h	646	209
Giant Mountain	<	9.4	6 h	930	210
Noonmark Mountain	<	10.8	5 h	578	211
Bald Peak: East Trail	<	12.4	5 h 30	740	212

ADIRONDACKS	Level of difficulty	Total distance (km)	Time	Change of altitude (m)	Page
Gilligan Mountain	✓	3.6	1 h 30	204	212
Poke-o-Moonshine	✓	3.8	2 h	390	213
Haystack Mountain	✓✓	10.6	4 h	377	214
Scarface Mountain	✓✓	10.4	4 h 15	450	215
Mount Baker	✓	2.8	1 h 30	274	215
Ampersand Mountain	✓✓	8.8	3 h 45	541	216
Whiteface Mountain: Trail to Whiteface	✓✓✓	16.6	7 h	1103	217
Catamount Mountain	✓✓	5.8	2 h 45	466	218
Silver Lake Mountain	✓	3	1 h 30	275	219
LONG HIKES					
Mount Marcy: Van Hoevenberg Trail	✓✓	23.6	2 days	965	221
Mount Marcy: Trail to the High Peak	✓✓✓	29.1	2 days	1165	223
Mount Haystack	✓✓✓	28.5	2 days	1048	224
Dix Mountain	✓✓✓	21.9	2 days	975	225
Gothics	✓✓	21.8	2 days	910	226

GLOSSARY

■ Hiking Vocabulary

Bergschrund:	a crevasse or gap at the head of a glacier, also called rimaye
Bivouac:	a temporary open camp without tents
Cairn:	a pile of rough stones arranged at the summit, or along a trail indicating the way
Chimney:	narrow vertical fissure in a rock-face, used by climbers to ascend
Cirque:	a deep bowl-shaped hollow with steep sides and a sloping floor formed by glaciers, also called a corrie
Col, Pass:	a depression in the ridge connecting two mountains, often providing a pass from one slope to another
Crest:	the top of a mountain
Crevasse:	a deep open crack, usually in a glacier
Dièdre:	a large shallow corner in a rock face
Gully:	a water-worn ravine, through which avalanches pass
Knob:	a small rounded hill or knoll
Ledge:	a narrow shelf-like rock projection from a mountain or side of a cliff
Massif:	a compact group of mountain
Marker:	anything indicating the trail to follow such as paint markings on trees or rocks

Moraine: a mass of rocks and debris carried by glaciers and forming ridges when deposited

Névé: an expanse of porous, granular snow, not yet formed into ice at the head of a glacier, also called firn

Overhang: the overhanging part of a rock formation on a cliff or mountainside

Pitch: the steepness of a mountain slope over a distance

Ridge   the intersection between two rock faces

Scree: the small loose stones that accumulates at the foot of a cliff or slope

Serac: a steep pointed tower of ice among crevasses on a glacier

Through-route: the horizontal progression across a rock face

Timberline: tree-growth limit above which trees are less than 2 m high

RECOMMENDED READING

THE ADIRONDACK MOUNTAIN CLUB, *Guide to Adirondack Trails / High Peaks Region*, editor Tony Goodwin, 1994, 324 p.

APPALACHIAN MOUNTAIN CLUB, *AMC Maine Mountain Guide*, 1992, 306 p.

APPALACHIAN MOUNTAIN CLUB, *AMC White Mountain Guide*, 1992, 638 p.

DOAN, Daniel, *Fifty Hikes in the White Mountains*, Backcountry Publications, 1994, 220 p.

GANGE, Jared, *Hiker's Guide to the Mountains of Vermont*, Huntingdon Graphics, 96 p.

THE GREEN MOUNTAIN CLUB, *Long Trail Guide, Vermont Hiking Trails Series*, 1996, 237 p.

THE GREEN MOUNTAIN CLUB, *Day Hiker's Guide to Vermont*, 1987, 180 p.

THE GREEN MOUNTAIN CLUB, *Fifty Hikes in Vermont*, Backcountry Publications, 1994, 190 p.

PETERSON, Roger Tory, *Peterson's Field Guide: All the Birds of Eastern and Central North America*, Houghton Mifflin, 1994

INDEX

Travel Notes _____

Travel Notes _____

Travel Notes _____

Travel Notes

Travel Notes _____

Travel Notes _____

Travel Notes _____

Travel Notes _____

Travel Notes _____

Travel Notes _____

Travel Notes _____

■ ULYSSES TRAVEL GUIDES

☐ Affordable Bed & Breakfasts
  in Québec .... $11.95 CAN
                    $9.95 US
☐ Canada's Maritime
  Provinces............... $24.95 CAN
                 $14.95 US
☐ Cuba .... $24.95 CAN
                 $16.95 US
☐ Dominican Republic. $24.95 CAN
                 $16.95 US
☐ El Salvador............. $22.95 CAN
                 $14.95 US
☐ Guadeloupe........... $24.95 CAN
                 $16.95 US
☐ Honduras .... $24.95 CAN
                 $16.95 US
☐ Martinique.............. $24.95 CAN
                 $16.95 US
☐ Montréal .... $19.95 CAN
                 $13.95 US
☐ Nicaragua .... $24.95 CAN
                 $16.95 US
☐ Ontario .... $24.95 CAN
                 $14.95 US
☐ Panamá .... $24.95 CAN
                 $16.95 US
☐ Portugal................. $24.95 CAN
                 $16.95 US
☐ Provence -
  Côte d'Azur .... $24.95 CAN
                 $14.95 US
☐ Québec................. $24.95 CAN
                 $14.95 US

☐ Toronto .... $18.95 CAN
                 $13.95 US
☐ Vancouver .... $14.95 CAN
                 $10.95 US
☐ Western Canada....... $24.95 CAN
                 $16.95 US

■ ULYSSES GREEN ESCAPES

☐ Hiking in the Northeastern
  United States....... $19.95 CAN
                 $13.95 US
☐ Hiking in Québec ..... $19.95 CAN
                 $13.95 US

■ ULYSSES DUE SOUTH

☐ Cartagena (Colombia) . $9.95 CAN
                 $5.95 US
☐ Montelimar (Nicaragua) $9.95 CAN
                 $5.95 US
☐ Puerto Plata - Sosua - Cabarete
  (Dominican Republic) .... $9.95 CAN
                 $5.95 US
☐ Puerto Vallarta .... $14.95 CAN
  (Mexico) $9.95 US
☐ St. Barts.................... $9.95 CAN
                 $7.95 US
☐ St. Martin .... $9.95 CAN
                 $7.95 US

■ ULYSSES TRAVEL JOURNAL

☐ Ulysses Travel Journal $9.95 CAN
                 $7.95 US

QUANTITY	TITLES	PRICE	TOTAL
	Sub-total		
NAME:_____	Postage & Handling	$4.00	
ADDRESS:_____	Sub-total		
_____	G.S.T.in Canada 7%		
_____	TOTAL		

_____

Payment: ☐ Money Order ☐ Visa ☐ MasterCard
Card Number:_____
Expiry Date:_____
Signature_____

ULYSSES TRAVEL PUBLICATIONS
4176 Rue Saint-Denis, Montréal, Québec, H2W 2M5
☎(514) 843-9447 fax (514) 843-9448